BORN *Three* TIMES

A New Life, A New Liver, A New Love

Frieda S. Dixon

Inspiring Voices books may be ordered through booksellers or by contacting:

Inspiring Voices
1663 Liberty Drive
Bloomington, IN 47403
www.inspiringvoices.com
1-(866) 697-5313

ISBN: 978-1-4624-0387-5 (sc)
ISBN: 978-1-4624-0388-2 (e)

Library of Congress Control Number: 2012920036

Printed in the United States of America

Inspiring Voices rev. date: 10/29/2012

Dedication

To my sister, Audrey Kimmel, who has known me the longest and loves me anyway. We have walked much of the same path in life and have been there for each other through thick and thin. Love you, Middle Sis.

"Let this be written for a future generation; that a people not yet created may praise the Lord" (Psalms 102:18).

Rick Warren echoes this thought in his book, *The Purpose Driven Life*: "You owe it to future generations to preserve the testimony of how God helped you to fulfill his purposes on earth. It is a witness that will continue to speak long after you are in heaven."

All Scripture verses are from the NIV, New International Version of the Bible.

Acknowledgements

*M*y sister, Audrey Kimmel, who critiqued my manuscript and provided valuable input about people and family events that helped my fuzzy memory.

Theresa Anderson, a fellow member of the Christian Authors Guild in Woodstock, Georgia, and my writing coach. As an objective reader, Theresa was able to point out the changes I needed to make in flow and sentence structure and helped me change the dreaded passive sentences that I like to write. She also critiqued by book and urged me to publish it to encourage others who experience difficult times.

Diana Baker, a founder of the Christian Authors Guild, who edited my book three times and found all the punctuation and grammatical mistakes that I overlooked.

My friends, Julia LaBeauve and Shane & Cassie Williams, who used their professional camera to shoot my picture for the back cover.

My girlfriends, Shirley Bobo and Libby Garrison, who encouraged me to tell my story while I still have a clear mind and a good memory.

My supportive husband, Charles, who pushed me to write my life story and washed lots of dishes so I could keep my head in the computer.

Tanya Hall, my publicist, who is learning with me how to market my book.

Introduction

*E*veryone who sees my cranberry glass collection admires its beauty. Each piece of the shimmering, rose-colored glass, whether large or small, is pleasing to the eye. When gathered together in a group, the various shapes and sizes make quite a statement.

My fascination with cranberry glass began when I shopped in the quaint town of Stone Mountain, Georgia. As I browsed through the antique shops and gift boutiques, a beautiful rose-colored glass basket caught my eye. It was love at first sight but the price was way beyond my budget to purchase. The proprietor agreed to put the basket on layaway, and after three months, I took my extravagant purchase home.

I am a connoisseur of the beauty of blown glass and am equally fascinated by how it is made. During a trip to the Fenton Glass Factory in West Virginia, I learned that craftsmen take the raw materials for making basic glass and add selenium oxide to make a red glass mixture. Once molten, the red liquid is blown into various shapes and sizes of ruby glass—dark red and pretty, but lacking luster. The recipe for creating shimmering, cranberry glass requires an important added step—the addition of gold. When heated, the gold is dispersed turning the ruby-red mixture into an opalescent, rose-colored liquid. The craftsman then blows, shapes, stretches, and crimps the blob of transformed glass into cranberry baskets, vases, and pitchers. Each piece passes through many skillful hands before it is cured and ready for service. The dispersed gold is visible throughout the finished product, reflecting light and allowing light to pass through. This delicate and detailed process guarantees that each cranberry piece is unique, stamped with the seal of the artist who created it.

I acquired most of my cranberry glass over a twenty-year period when I was struggling to survive. As I built my collection, God was at work in my life, turning my tears into laughter and my mourning to joy. The skillful hands of my Creator formed and shaped my life as I experienced the red-hot heat of many difficult circumstances. As the glassblower gives life to each molten blob, God blew new life into me during each step of my journey. His presence was dispersed in my life like the gold that is added to the ruby liquid, and I bear His mark. Now it is up to me to let others see Him through the way I live.

"But he knows the way that I take; and when he has tested me,
I will come forth as gold" (Job 23:10).

—Frieda Dixon

Part One

"Before I formed you in the womb I knew you, before you were born,
I set you apart…" (Jeremiah 1:5).

CHAPTER 1

~

Flashing Lights

They say your whole life flashes before you when you are facing death, but I couldn't remember anything about the past—I was only praying for a future.

"This is Debbie, your transplant coordinator. We think we found a donor liver. We need you at the hospital in two hours."

"What did you say?" I shouted into the phone. I had been led to believe by my team of doctors that it would be a long time before my name would rise to the top of the transplant list. I often doubted that this day would come and wondered if I had used up my allotment of second chances.

"We think we found a match," Debbie calmly explained. "And remember, we need you to come in fasting so we can prep you for surgery."

That phone call abruptly changed my routine Wednesday afternoon into a frantic race for time. An adrenaline rush kicked my sluggish mind and body into high gear. "Dear God, help me," I said aloud. Since I was alone, no one else heard my plea.

I needed to find Charles, my husband, who was attending a meeting somewhere in the plant at Lockheed Martin Aerospace Company. God answered my prayer when the name of the project engineer he was seeing suddenly popped into my mind. About that same time, the doorbell rang announcing my friend Marianne, who had said earlier that she might come for a visit that afternoon. She hugged me and bounced with joy when I told her the news. I wished I could have shared her enthusiasm, but I was too nervous and scared.

Somehow, we managed to get a message through to Charles and call my other family members and my pastor. Marianne threw some personal items into my suitcase, put away the food I was preparing for supper, and had me ready to go when Charles came through the door.

My heart pounded and my stomach churned as we drove to Emory University Hospital. Afternoon rush-hour traffic was building as we made our way onto the perimeter around Atlanta. My anxiety level rose further as cars and eighteen-wheelers slowed to a crawl. The thought that this might be my last ride entered my mind.

Debbie greeted me with a hug and smile as I walked through the double doors into the hospital lobby. I tried to smile back at her, but all I really wanted to do was cry. She escorted us to admissions, where I signed a stack of paperwork, and then to the lab for blood work, an EKG, and other essential tests to see if I was still healthy enough for the arduous surgery. After my medical workup, my husband and I settled into my room on the pre-transplant floor of the hospital, nervously waiting for what tomorrow would bring.

"Mrs. Dixon, do you realize that once we remove your diseased liver you will die unless we successfully graft in a new organ?" the transplant doctor asked me later that evening.

"What other choices do I have?" I tried to joke as I signed the document granting permission for what would be life-ending or life-giving surgery.

My married sons, Stuart and Michael, arrived before midnight and settled into the uncomfortable chairs in my private room. Everyone dozed, only to be jarred awake by the deafening sound of a helicopter and its bright flashing lights outside my sixth story window. The clock read 3:00 am.

"Maybe that's my new liver," I said aloud, but also as a prayer.

I lay in my bed listening to my heart beat in rhythm with the ticking of the wall clock. *Were these the last minutes of my life?* The mild snoring of my husband and sons was irritating. *How can they sleep at a time like this?* To take my mind off myself, I thought about the unnamed family who had made a courageous decision to donate their loved one's organs while dealing with their own personal grief. I prayed for my donor family and all the other patients in the hospital. War correspondent Ernie Pyle is often credited with saying, "There are no atheists in foxholes." I doubted there were many atheists on the pre-transplant floor on May 12, 1998 either.

During those early morning hours while my family drifted in and out of sleep, I reflected on my fifty-four years of life and the difficult journey that had brought me to this watershed moment. It had always been my desire to make a difference in the lives of others and accomplish something worthwhile with my life. However, many of my goals and ambitions from early childhood and young adulthood had been put on the back burner or cut short. I struggled emotionally and spiritually during those years as I tried to make sense of the circumstances of my life. Due to an eighteen-year battle with liver disease, my middle adulthood years were the most challenging as I fought to survive physically. Only with a successful liver transplant could I have a second chance at life and the opportunity to enjoy better health.

At 5:00 am, bright overhead lights rudely interrupted my thoughts and awakened my family. The nursing team entered my room. "We're taking you to surgery," the RN announced as she injected a brain numbing drug into my IV.

My family followed my gurney to the elevator where I mouthed one final "I love you." The doors closed, and the elevator began a slow descent to the first floor. My chance for a future was sitting in a red and white cooler just beyond the closed double doors of the surgical suite.

My transplant surgeon's eyes were all I could see of his masked face. "I will see you in recovery," he optimistically said. The anesthesiologist announced that he was starting my IV drip. As I drifted into unconsciousness, I prayed I would live so I could tell my story about the unseen, divine hand that had pushed and pulled me through life—testing, yet encouraging me to keep on keeping on.

CHAPTER 2

❧

High Falls

*M*y childhood retreat was a secret place accessed only by a rocky path hidden among evergreen and maple trees. There was no marker on the road or any way to know an oasis was there unless a local revealed the path to the falls hidden behind a white-steeple church. The falls were wider than they were high, and no one knew how High Falls got its name. The swimming hole at the base of the falls was constantly replenished by the cold water that rushed over the precipice of smooth rock. It was a perfect spot to escape the summer heat. In winter the roaring falls became a trickle before freezing in place like an icy statue. For months it silently endured the bitterly cold and shortened days, patiently waiting for the thaws of spring to set it free from its hibernation.

My hometown in upstate New York boasted one stop sign that marked where two streets intersected. Dairy cows and farm silos outnumbered the people in this small agricultural community. A two-room schoolhouse, Cooper's Store, and the Wesleyan Methodist Church were prominent features on Main Street. Victorian style houses with wrap-around porches lined the side streets, some lovingly cared for and others allowed to deteriorate to a shabbiness that made you want to move in and fix them up. Maple Street was a fitting name for a street with sidewalks and huge sturdy trees that produced sticky, sweet sap in the spring and glorious yellow and crimson leaves to welcome the fall.

It was on this street in Burke, New York that I was born and lived until I was six years old. Many of my early memories revolve around events in our small gray house at the end of Maple Street. A big porch wrapped around the front door of the house. Large vegetable and flower gardens replaced the grass in the side yards. At the bottom of a steep drop-off behind the house, a brook gurgled its way over stones and stumps. The school, church, post office, general store, and my grandparents' house were all within walking distance. In that rural village my character would be shaped and my personality formed.

CHAPTER 3

~

Fifi Minnow

Frieda Mildred Schryer was a long, complex name for such a small, frail baby. I was five pounds dripping wet when they weighed me at the hospital in Malone, five miles southwest of Burke. I arrived as the third and final child of Frederick and Mildred Schryer on February 8, 1944. They say the snowdrifts reached the telephone wires the day I was born. That was certainly possible since there were no hills or mountains to slow the blasts of icy air that swept across the Canadian border into the North Country of New York State.

My impending arrival was so well hidden by my mother's full house dresses, I was a big surprise—more like a shock—to my older sisters. At my house, discussions of birth and the mysteries surrounding it were avoided, especially in the presence of children. Janice Marilyn was ten when I arrived in the world. She already had a sister eighteen months younger in Audrey Ann and didn't feel the need for another one. In all probability, they considered me more a doll than a baby. But since I was colicky, I soon convinced my sisters with my non-stop crying that I was for real.

Dad's very practical German lineage required a son to carry on the family name. Of course, I don't remember his disappointment, but my older sisters tell me he was none too happy about my arrival. His first choice of a name for me was Fredericka, but, thankfully, someone intervened and suggested Frieda. Finally, he agreed that Frieda was the closest thing he could think of to Fred, Jr. Mother liked the name Fifi because she had strong French Canadian roots and it seemed to fit me, since I was small like a poodle. The neighbors said I was so little I looked like a minnow. They combined the name Fifi with Minnow, and Fifi Minnow was my nickname from that point on.

In my little yellow-trimmed basinet, tucked into the corner of the dining room, I was oblivious to the swirl of history-making world events reported each day on the radio. D-Day was still four months away. Many men in our small town were soldiers in the Pacific, and an uncle was missing in action somewhere in Europe. Since Dad worked for an industry vital to the war effort, he stayed on the home front. I never would have been born if my father had been called into military service. Janice and Audrey remember ration coupons, victory gardens, and life-altering telegrams from the War Department, as well as dancing in the streets on VE and VJ Day. As for me, I cried, nursed, and slept through it all.

Fifi Minnow Age One

CHAPTER 4

Minnie and Fred

My father, Frederick Schryer, was raised in Burke as the oldest son of eight children. His formal education ended in eighth grade when he found a job to help support the family. He and his four brothers were not encouraged to graduate from high school because the men of the family were expected to work with their hands. A high school diploma was not considered essential for manual labor. His three sisters, on the other hand, were required to graduate from high school and go on to college since females in the Schryer family were encouraged to become teachers. My father's financial support for the family involved helping his sisters get a college education. He was also expected to hunt and fish to put food on the table.

When not working, he met his friends at the local tavern for drinks and companionship. My father loved to hunt, fish, and pitch for the local softball team. He carried me around in his pack basket when he went fishing, hoping that I would share his interests. None of it rubbed off on me.

When I was five, Dad invited for supper a Mohawk Indian friend who worked with him at the aluminum plant in Massena, New York.

His co-workers and friends admired my father's work ethic and values. He was a trustworthy, loyal friend, and a perfectionist who was never satisfied with his work. Fred was also known for his temper when things didn't turn out as expected. For days I was excited about the friend's visit but was very disappointed when the "Indian" arrived not wearing any feathers.

My mother, Mildred Miller or Minnie, was raised on a farm near Malone. She learned to do chores, garden, and cook—but was hampered by chronic asthma. Whooping cough at an early age had damaged her lungs, so any infection was serious. She met my father as a teenager, but left Malone to go down state to Brockport Normal School near Rochester to earn her teaching certificate. She, too, believed a good education was of utmost importance for females. After graduation she taught history at Webster Central School while keeping up a correspondence with my father back in Burke. At age twenty-five, she cut short her teaching career to return to Burke to marry my father. Married women did not normally teach school at that time, so like other wives in that small town, most of Mother's daily energy was spent in the kitchen and garden, planning and working to prepare the next meal. She always found the time and energy to bake homemade banana bread and take one of her delicious casseroles to a sick neighbor or family member.

Minnie and Fred were hard-working folks who always seemed to have trouble making ends meet. They married in 1933 at the height of the Great Depression. It wasn't an easy time for them. Their marriage was severely tested during the relentless years of the economic downturn. The only work that was available for my father was sporadic and out of town, leaving Mother to raise my two older sisters with the help of grandparents. It wasn't until much later in life that I would understand how the struggles of those years colored their view of life. My parents were mismatched in many ways. My father was tall and athletic—my mother short in stature and short of breath with no interest in sports; my father had little formal education—my mother had a teaching degree; my father preferred to hunt, fish, and drink with the boys— my mother chose to content herself with domestic duties and the 4H Club. And she didn't believe in strong drink. Their personality differences and financial struggles significantly affected our family life and influenced my childhood experiences.

CHAPTER 5

✦

Sister Siblings

*B*ecause Janice and Audrey were ten and eight years older, they had much responsibility for my care and upbringing. Many times my mother didn't feel well enough to keep up with the demands of a small baby or busy toddler. My sisters helped me learn to walk by fastening a small harness about my waist and chest. Once I was mobile, I loved to drag my red vinyl dog around on a string, sit in the small rocker my Father built for me, and play with a large ceramic bunny given to me on Easter. I named that bunny, Deacon Babcock, after the Methodist Church minister. My favorite game was Button-Button and I constantly begged my sisters to play it with me. I never tired of them hiding a big button in the book shelves, on the windowsills, or under a sofa pillow and then announcing, "Button-button whose got the button." I looked all over and after I found the button, begged them to play again.

Janice and Audrey wore pigtails or braids as we call them today. We all wore jumpers with cotton blouses, which was very much the fashion in our part of the country in the 1940s. My family was fortunate in that we could live off the land. We had large gardens and extended family in the area that helped to harvest the fruits of our labors. All of us girls had to help with the gardens and canning, but much more was expected from my older sisters than from me.

Whatever free time Janice and Audrey enjoyed after garden and kitchen duty involved the care and maintenance of me. Our small village offered little in the way of entertainment, but my sisters could walk up Maple Street to Main Street and find girlfriends or cousins to play with. Often they had to take me along in my carriage or stroller and come home sooner than they wanted because I was crying and hungry again. As I got older, they loved to play school on the front porch with me as their willing student. But they still didn't like having a tag-a-long sister when they walked to town to meet their friends. They made me believe that the dragonflies that flew around the brook behind the house were "darning needles" that would sew my lips together if I tattled on them.

CHAPTER 6

Kissing Kin

Growing up in Burke meant being surrounded by lots of family. My relatives comprised around ten percent of the village population of three hundred people. Ground Zero for my father's family was the big white Victorian house on Main Street.

Grandma Schryer was the glue that held the whole family together. Everyone flocked to my grandparents' house on Saturday night for my Grandma's homemade baked beans, rolls, and fruit pies. During the week her donut jar was filled with mouth-watering, deep fried delights waiting to be eaten by anyone who stopped by for coffee and some advice. My white-haired, sturdily-built grandmother was never idle. Cooking, canning, washing, and caring for her multitude of children and grandchildren occupied much of her time.

When spring and summer days replaced the icy days of late winter, Grandma was in her garden tending her vegetables and colorful flowers. Bouquets of purple, rose, white, and pink sweet peas adorned the dining room table during the short growing season of July and August. She liked to dress as colorfully as her flowers. Her bright house dresses were always in style, and when she went shopping or to church, she dressed to the nines with matching hats and gloves. I can still picture her sitting in her big chair in the living room reading her Bible during those few moments when she could relax.

My father's brothers and sisters lived within walking distance, and with their large families of four and five kids each, there was no shortage of cousins. My favorite place to play with my cousins was on the wide, wrap-around porch of my grandparents' big house. We played school, dressed dolls, pretended to be cowboys and Indians, and established home base for the endless games of Hide and Seek and Kick the Can. On really hot days, we raced to High Falls with a large towel and a picnic basket full of homemade goodies. We splashed in the waist-high pool, ran under the falls, and sunned ourselves on the large flat rocks.

Playing with my cousins gave me my first experiences in social relationships. The oldest cousins had to look out for the younger ones. The older ones could be quite bossy, and the younger ones like me didn't like it. There was always some rivalry or squabble, but we learned to resolve most of our differences without adult intervention. When a cousin decided to tattle-tale to their parents, the adults took sides and feelings got hurt and feathers got ruffled.

My mother's family lived in Malone, five miles east of Burke, and was much smaller in number—but just as boisterous. Mother's sister, Gert, married an optometrist who had inherited family money. She and Uncle Paul owned a modern house in Malone and a rustic cabin on Indian Lake. Aunt Gert was a very jolly person who was a real contrast to my serious-minded mother.

Spending the night at her house and especially at the lake cabin was a treat. My three Soper cousins and I had many fun times playing Ping-Pong and other games on the big screened-in porch—as well as swimming and boating in the lake. My cousins called me Fifi Minnow and took a special interest in my health and welfare. Like my mother, I had allergies and asthma which flared up whenever I visited the Soper's musty lake house.

There was often tension between our family and the Soper family. Our financial and political differences were often discussed at home.

On more than one occasion, I heard my father criticize the Sopers as being too rich for their own good and call them "died-in-the-wool" Republicans. This meant that no amount of reason would change their minds when it came to politics. Since my father was a common man, a little guy who struggled to make ends meet, he and my mother prided themselves on being New Deal Democrats and big fans of Franklin and Eleanor Roosevelt.

CHAPTER 7

The Sugar Social

My school and church were special places where I excelled and felt good about myself. In the village of Burke you were Methodist, Presbyterian, or Catholic. Every Sunday the Methodist church bell rang for fifteen minutes giving everyone time to walk to town. I loved the beautiful stained glass windows in that small church on Main Street. During the Sunday service, I would lie down on the church pew and think about the Bible stories depicted on those windows. Our Sunday school class met in the church basement, and it was there I received my first introduction to the love of God and Jesus. My grandmother and aunts always made sure I went to Sunday school each week and were an early religious influence in my life.

The two-room schoolhouse I attended for first and second grades stood far back from the road across the street from my grandparent's house. Maple trees stood like soldiers on either side of the long walkway leading to the entrance. My parents enrolled me in school when I was five-years old and the same age as one of my cousins. He and I were the only students in the first grade class. I loved to read and write, and since my cousin struggled to do both, the teacher assigned me to help him. He didn't like it one bit, but I was hooked. From then on, I knew I wanted to be a teacher.

All the Burke kids walked to school, and the changing seasons made those walks unique and adventuresome. In the fall, the abundant trees that lined every street in town dropped a colorful, crunchy carpet for us to kick and run through. The shorter days of late fall were greeted by the first Canadian snows. For the next five months, I waddled to school bundled up in a heavy coat, scarf, leggings, boots, and mittens. From November through April, the stove heater in the middle of the school room was covered with ice-crusted mittens and surrounded by dripping snow boots.

Playing with my cousins in the winter was as much fun as in the summer. Sometimes there were ten or twelve of us running through my grandparents' house. When they'd had enough of us noisy kids, we were told to bundle up and go outside to play. We built snow forts and played house under the snow laden branches of the fir trees in the yard. The melting snow on the roof created icicles as big as stalactites hanging from the eves of the porch. We broke off icicles and sucked on them like Popsicles, completely ignoring the roof soot imbedded inside.

Every winter I eagerly looked forward to the Methodist Church "sugar social." It usually took place in March when a plentiful supply of clean, fluffy snow was still on the ground. Starting in February, tree sap was collected in metal buckets. The buckets were attached with spouts bored into the trunks of the abundant sugar maples. I interrupted my walks to school, church, or my grandparents' house to stop at each tree with a bucket. When no one was looking, I'd take off my mitten, stick my finger in the sticky juice, and relish the sweet nectar. It was a sample of delicious days to come.

After the sap was gathered by the farmers, it was taken into the woods to the sugar shack to be boiled down into maple syrup. The springtime social was a celebration of another successful year of "sugaring off." The cooking started days before. Pea soup, baked beans, glazed donuts, and fried salt pork were served to all who gathered in the church hall. As the mouth-watering feast concluded, I knew the best was waiting in the wings. Like Santa Claus arriving with his pack of gifts, the men of the church burst through the doors with big pans of fresh packed snow. Hot maple syrup was drizzled in bacon shaped ribbons on top of the snow. When cooled, the syrup strips turned to a delicious taffy treat that we scooped up with a wooden stick.

CHAPTER 8

Mystery Brother

My many happy memories of my childhood in Burke are tinged by times of unhappiness, which I was too young to understand. In my parents' generation, personal and family secrets were often kept in the dark. In the small town of Burke, it seemed that everybody, including my sisters, knew about our half-brother except me. My unmarried mother gave birth to John A. (Jack) Miller in April 1926 when she was seventeen years old.

The details surrounding Jack's birth and upbringing are few and far between, except to say that after he was born, my mother moved on with her life. While she earned a teaching degree at Brockport Normal School and taught in the Webster Central school system, Jack was raised by my maternal grandparents and Aunt Gert. My father was introduced to my mother in 1927 by one of his sisters after Jack was born. My parents corresponded while Mother was in teachers' college, but their letters never made any mention of Jack and the circumstances of his birth. There was a lot of gossip in town and none of it in my mother's favor. According to a poem written by my father to my mother prior to their marriage, he was under a lot of pressure not to marry her.

Frederick Schryer's Poem to Mildred Miller (Milly)
Written between 1930 and 1933

Her Past

They say she's not the girl for me
They say she's not true blue,
They talk of what she used to be,
And things she used to do.

They corner me and tell me why,
She'd never made a wife,
They shake their heads and heave a sign,
And talk of her past life.

But what is past is past, I guess
They're not the ones to judge;
I'll never love her one bit less
Because they hold a grudge.

I looked a little deeper and
I've found a lot that's fine,
And though they have put on her a brand,
I'm proud to call her mine.

Her past is like an open book
That they all may see and read.
Every one may take a look,
At the life she used to lead.

Step up you hypocrites and see,
A woman that's true blue,
She's plenty good enough for me,
And far too good for you.

Let he among you without sin,
Just cast the first word stone.
You are no better than she has been,
So leave her past alone.

I've chosen her to share my lot;
To sit at my right hand.
Her love for me rubs out the blot;
Because I understand.

—Frederick Schryer

When I was born, Jack was already eighteen years old. While we lived in Burke, he was a frequent visitor to our house. If anyone talked about his relationship to our family, I was too young to understand. I am not sure if it was because my father insisted that Jack's identity not be revealed or because my mother was too embarrassed and in denial about his origins. Janice and Audrey were closer to Jack's age, so they had more in common with him. But I remember him playing games with me and drawing funny pictures for me to color. He was a very artistic and creative person with a delightful sense of humor that kept everyone laughing at his silly antics. He could mimic just about any sound or person and keep us well entertained with his voices and stories.

The lingering gossip regarding my mother, along with her worsening asthmatic condition, led our family away from Burke when I was six years old. Janice was seventeen at the time and about to enter her senior year of high school in Malone. She did not want to move to a new school, so my parents agreed to let her live with Aunt Gert in Malone for a year until she graduated. Since Audrey was sixteen and a rising high school junior, she moved with the family. It was not easy for her to leave her friends and start over in another school.

At that time, my father had a steady job at the American Aluminum Company in Massena, where he was a well-respected foreman. My father constantly fretted about giving up that position, the best one he would ever have, for a promised job in his brother's business in Rochester, NY. He was the first born and favorite son of the eight children in his family. It was difficult for him to move away from his parents and the woods and mountains of the Adirondack region. But my mother remembered her healthier days when she was in teachers' college down state in Webster, New York and wanted to move back there. She could be pretty persuasive when she wanted something.

Even though my family was deeply rooted in the North Country of New York State, we packed our possessions and sold the little house on Maple Street. But like a siren song, Burke would call my father and the rest of our family back to our roots for the rest of our lives.

Chapter 9

"W" is for Webster

"Webster–Where Life is Worth Living" was engraved on all the signs that led to this bustling village where our family hoped to forge a new future. This suburban community of Rochester, New York was three miles from Lake Ontario. Residents enjoyed the cool breezes blowing off the lake in summer and endured the endless rounds of lake effect snow in the winter.

Webster's Main Street was home to many family owned businesses including Tinkelpaugh's Funeral Home, Whitmer's General Store, Papanaugh's Candy Kitchen, and Hank Herbst's Soda Fountain. Webster Central School on South Avenue, made of red brick and built in the shape of a "W," was at the center of village life. "The intelligence of the people is the security of the nation" was engraved over the front entrance of the school. This quote from Daniel Webster, the namesake of the village, was considered a sacred duty to be carried out by my family and my teachers.

Webster Central School was just a few short blocks from where we settled on South Avenue. That school became my second home until I graduated in 1961. The two-room schoolhouse in Burke was replaced by multiple classes of third graders. I was in heaven–new teachers, new friends, a new church, and lots of kids to play with that were not my cousins. Books, school supplies, homework, and the school library made each day special for me. I thrived in that environment.

Those of us who walked to school were called "townies," but some of my best friends were "out of townies" and rode the school buses. As a townie, I was afforded certain pleasures while walking to school–kicking the colorful, crunchy leaves in October, slipping and sliding on the ice covered sidewalks in January, and discovering the first buds on the trees and bushes in April. Sometimes a boy might walk me home from school and carry my books. I wasn't dependent on any transportation other than my two feet to get me to the soda fountain and Candy Kitchen. With my twenty-five cent allowance, I could buy a nickel Coke or ice cream cone and still have money to spare.

However, I was insecure about where I lived and believed that "townies" like me were at the bottom of the popularity pecking order. I longed for the greener grass on the other side of the fence and for a yellow and black bus to take me to a pretty house on the outskirts of town. In my perfect world, I had another thirty minutes every morning and afternoon to giggle with girlfriends or steal a glance at some cute boy—hoping that one day he'd save me a seat. In my imagination, the bus would stop on a quiet street in front of a modern house with a well-manicured lawn and I would go home to bliss.

During the ten years I lived in Webster, my family frequently visited Burke and Malone. It was always fun to see my cousins and splash in the refreshing water of High Falls, but I couldn't wait to get back to Webster. My opportunities and horizons were greatly expanded in that suburban environment. I would blossom in this new world, whereas my parents' financial and health struggles were only made worse.

Webster W-Shaped School

CHAPTER 10

Mickey's on the Moose

O ur house was a converted second floor apartment in a small grey Victorian on a corner lot one-quarter mile from the school. Weeds infested the large yard and flower beds, and the paint was in a constant state of peeling. Most Novembers a deer buck, shot on one of my father's hunting trips, was hung by his antlers in our half of the garage. To make matters worse, our apartment on South Avenue was on the same road as the school. Since this was a main street into town, I was self-conscious about where I lived.

A steep flight of stairs led to a storage room landing and the entrance to our five-room apartment decorated with "early attic" furnishings. Function and serviceability were the criteria when our furniture was brought through the front door. Our tables, chairs, dressers, and end tables were well nicked and worn and stained with water spots and rings. A cigarette or pipe burn could be found on most of them. Doilies covered the tops and arms of the furniture pieces in an attempt to keep them from harm. When the doilies were removed, dusty patterns that looked like snowflakes decorated the surface. The kitchen and bathroom had been installed in the pre-war era and were hot in summer and cold in winter. My bedroom retreat was decorated with pink and grey bedding, agonizingly chosen from the Montgomery Ward catalog. I had saved my hard earned babysitting money for the perfect ensemble.

Our dining room was the center of family activity and not just for meals. It was an all-purpose room in the center of the apartment. A large oak pedestal table occupied the center, surrounded by six captains' chairs. My father's bed was in one corner of the dining room, and Esmerelda's turtle house and Mickey's bird cage occupied the bay window niche. The turtle stayed confined, but the bright green parakeet was often loose and flying from room to room. Two deer heads mounted in the living room served as the bird's perfect perch. My father taught that parakeet to squawk "Mickey's on the Moose." My mother's hot, dusty bedroom was adjacent to the dining room. The bird feathers and dust didn't help her asthma, and I too had allergy issues living in that environment.

A small upright desk sat in one corner of the dining room. It's stained walnut color and outward appearance was nothing to brag about. It stood off the floor on four straight legs that balanced three large drawers with wooden knobs, and was topped by a sloped drop lid that hid the interior. When I was finally tall enough to open the drop lid and look inside, I was captivated. Eight mail slots and a shelf with a drawer underneath held all sorts of interesting pieces of paper and trinkets. The drop lid expanded the desk so that I could color and draw. Many days I played post office, secretary, or school teacher, putting letters in and out of the slots and organizing the trinkets in the drawer.

During my school years, the top of the desk became the home of our party line rotary phone. One ring was for the neighbors, and three rings meant the phone was for us. When I picked up the phone to call out, I often interrupted a neighbor's conversation and had to wait until they were done. And of course, we never knew who was listening to our calls. It was impossible to have a private conversation with a girl or boy friend until the phone company connected our town to private calling.

Many years after I left home, during preparation for a move, my mother asked me if there was anything in the house I wanted. For years I had coveted that desk and jumped at the opportunity to have it in my home. For me, it represented a more carefree, imaginative time in my life—a time when I was in charge and could organize the envelopes and pieces of paper in the various slots of my play office. Order and neatness were always important to me, and I could escape the clutter and confusion of our household by just pulling down that drop lid.

Standing– Audrey, Mother, Janice Seated – Father, Frieda

CHAPTER 11

The Blue Fairy

Mother had a nickname or saying for everything and everyone. The main figment of my mother's imagination was a creature she named the "Blue Fairy." This magical being was summoned whenever there was some unpleasant task or chore to do. "I'm waiting for the Blue Fairy to do the dishes," Mother would announce. "Where's the Blue Fairy when you need her?" she would ask. The fairy was no ordinary Tinkerbelle that flitted around and became annoying. In reality, the "Blue Fairy" was me! Instead of telling me to do the dishes, iron laundry, or go to the store, Mother implied that I'd better get busy or face the consequences.

"Matilda" was the name she used to describe my friends. When some well-off girl at school or on the street had a new dress, new bike, or new opportunity that I wished for, Mother put her in her place. "Matilda is spoiled because her father makes a lot of money. We can't keep up with Matilda's family, and besides you are a lot smarter," Mother would add. Once again, I was reminded that our family was on the low end of the financial totem pole. The names of "Rapunzel" and "Miss Muffett" were reserved for my siblings or cousins in a somewhat disparaging way.

One of Mother's favorite sayings was "The old grey mare ain't what she used to be." She used those words from an old folk song to describe herself when she felt too bad to get out of bed. It often meant that Dad and I were responsible for housework and cooking that day.

My mother was also a hummer and rocking chair rocker. Whenever she was idle, she hummmmm...ed. Put her in her rocking chair, and she hummmmm...ed in rhythm to the back and forth motion of the chair. I learned to tune the sound out and wouldn't hear it until a visiting friend asked about the noise.

Taking on voices for various characters in books was another of Mother's pastimes. She adopted the slave dialect of Brer Rabbit and Brer Fox as she read to me *The Tales of Uncle Remus* by Joel Chandler Harris. *The Fairy Tales of Hans Christian Andersen* provided Dutch characters that Mother imitated from *The Ugly Duckling* and *The Little Match Girl*. In typical childhood fashion, I was usually embarrassed by Mother's humming and flights of fantasy.

CHAPTER 12

~

My Escape

During the 1950s Webster thrived economically. It was a popular bedroom community for those who worked in Rochester during the heyday of Eastman Kodak, Bausch & Lomb, and the R.T. French Company. My parents hoped to benefit from the good economy of the region, but the prosperity of the Fifties was not evident at our house. My father's job with his brother did not go well and ended when I was in fourth grade. Dad's lack of education made it difficult for him to find steady work, which led him to bouts of depression. He missed his family in Burke and the rural lifestyle, as well as the Adirondack Mountains where he could hunt and fish.

My mother's health did not improve, but seemed to decline with the move to Webster. During my school years, she constantly battled asthmatic bronchitis, spending weeks in the hospital or bedridden at home. When Mother had one of her spells, I had to shop, cook, and keep house. On her really bad days, I skipped school to stay home with her while my father worked at whatever jobs he could find.

My mother and father constantly bickered and argued about one thing or another. Many times my parents' loud voices and my father's swearing woke me up in the morning as they argued in the kitchen. I knew the fight was over when my father stormed out of the kitchen and stomped down the back stairs by my bedroom window. Or my mother went crying to her bedroom and slammed the door.

Conflict seemed to center around my father's inability to find a good paying job. They often argued about money and my father's frequent trips back to Burke. Then my father brought up my mother's past and called her harsh names that were hard for me to understand. Those arguments made me feel insecure and inferior, and it was easy for me to get depressed. I'd often lie in bed and pray and wish I could have a normal home life like my friends.

Just like in Burke, church played an important role in my life. Even though my parents were church members, the next door neighbors usually made sure I was on time for Sunday school at the Webster Methodist Church. I loved my Sunday school class and our annual Vacation Church School and the teachers who planned crafts and handed out take home papers. During church, when I wasn't writing notes to my friends, I admired the Bible stories told by the beautiful stained glass windows. The cut glass pictures of Jesus blessing little children, stilling the storm on the Sea of Galilee, and His ascension into heaven comforted me. The meaning of those pictorial Bible stories found a place in my heart.

As I grew older, I liked to read biographies about people who overcame difficult circumstances and made a difference with their lives. Many of those stories were of men and women who credited God with their strength. My faith in God began to bud during those years, but it was many years before I learned to trust all my life circumstances into His hand. There was always a part of me that felt it was my responsibility to act and behave in such a way that God and Jesus would love me back. I didn't realize until much later in my life that God's love for me was unconditional.

My older sisters continually looked out for little Fifi Minnow. They were a buffer between me and my parents, so it was difficult for me when they left home. After spending a few months in college, Janice decided she wanted to go to work in Rochester. Once she had a way to support herself, she moved out of our Webster apartment. Audrey and I remained close and shared a room until she graduated from high school. Whenever Audrey's boyfriend, George Kimmel, came to visit, I made a real pest of myself. I hid behind the sofa and waited until he tried to steal a kiss, before jumping out and scaring them. George used to give me a dime to get lost. Even though we were eight years apart in age, Audrey and I were close and she was always there when I needed someone to talk to. Because my mother was uncomfortable discussing anything pertaining to sex, Audrey told me the facts of life and helped me during that period of time when I physically matured. I really missed our sisterly chats when Audrey returned to college.

I looked forward to spending time with Jack Miller, his wife Joyce, and their children when they visited us in Webster. After one visit, when I was a teenager, I went next door to the neighbor's house to see my friend, Helen. Her mother casually asked me how Jack was related to our family. I told her I thought he was an uncle or cousin, but that I would ask my mother.

Mother did not respond well to my inquiry. She started crying and accused our neighbor of being nosey and a gossip, and then she ran into her bedroom and slammed the door. I was mystified. What had I done to provoke such a reaction? Audrey was at home at the time, so I told her about the blowup and she went into Mother's room to talk to her. It became Audrey's responsibility to tell me the circumstances of Jack's birth and his relationship to me. I was warned not to ever discuss that matter with my parents and to never talk about it to anyone except the man I married. After seeing and hearing my mother's reaction, I vowed to keep the family "skeleton in the closet." Jack and my whole family suffered because my mother chose not to be open and up front about her past. But in the Forties and Fifties, it was a different time and those kinds of issues were left hidden. However, the undercurrent ran deep and was often the source of tension and arguments in our household.

Maybe it was to escape my home life that school and my personality found a perfect match. Most other kids my age seemed to lack my passion and were content to just get by when it came to grades. Not me! I excelled at everything and continually worked to be on top. In spite of their differences, my parents equally encouraged academic excellence. My mother loved school and history in particular. It came naturally to her to drill me for history tests and offer her opinions about my homework projects and papers. My father never advanced beyond eighth grade, but was a self-taught man who recognized the importance of education. He often tried to help me with my math homework, but his personal method of computation and the way it had to be done for school didn't match. I'd usually end up in tears and have to figure it out myself anyway. Regardless of family challenges we faced, my sisters and I were expected to excel in school and never settle for less than all A's.

Some people thought of me as the teacher's pet since I often found myself staying after school to help a teacher clean off the blackboards, sort papers, and sharpen pencils. Being within walking distance of the school turned out to be a great advantage. During the summers I worked in the school library. I shelved and checked out books, helped to make repairs, and was an all-around librarian's assistant. I loved the smell and feel of books and the words found in them. I was determined to get a good education so I could become a librarian or teacher.

Leading and organizing came easy to me. I could organize anything–homework assignments, the library card catalog, a school dance, and youth activities at church. You name it, I was in charge! But, I would be a nervous wreck until my undertaking came to fruition. After pulling off a great success, I was ready for another challenge. When people didn't want to do things my way, I was totally baffled and aggravated that they didn't want to follow my lead.

CHAPTER 13

~

Not for Wimps

After my older sisters left home, I was expected to help with more household duties. At my house the dirty clothes pile was always stacked high and the ironing basket ran over. On wash day I carried baskets of dirty clothes down three floors to the dingy, damp basement. The wash tubs and wringer washer sat in the corner near the bottom of the stairs. I hoped spiders or other creepy-crawling bugs had moved out and not set up housekeeping since the previous wash day.

I sorted the clothes by color and first put the whites, along with Tide and Clorox, into the round washing tub. After a twenty minute agitation, the water drained out. I lifted the soggy underwear with a wooden stick and fed the pieces one at a time through the hand-cranked wringer. Then after the rinse cycle, I fed the clothes again through the wringer allowing them to drop into the laundry basket. My father's work pants and shirts had to be starched. I dipped them into a pot of hot starch and water then put them through the wringer again. By this time more dirty clothes were agitating and the process started all over again.

Hanging up the clothes to dry depended on the season of the year and the weather. The basement clothes line was often full of clothes from the other tenants who lived in the house. It took several days to dry clothes indoors as opposed to those days where they could be hung outside and retrieved by nightfall. My father's starched work pants were dried on stretchers and those pants could almost stand on their own when taken off the line. On beautiful days when we could hang the clothes outside, the chore was lightened. I always hoped those clouds I saw in the sky didn't mean rain was coming. At the first sprinkle, I'd make a mad dash from the house to gather the clothes before they got wet all over again.

I am sure being in that basement for hours on end on wash day didn't help my mother's health. My allergies, too, reacted to the smell from the oil heater, the concrete dust on the floor, and the musty boxes full of stuff that were stored in the basement. Wash day was definitely not for wimps. But in spite of how bad my mother felt, she always made sure that we had clean clothes and good food to eat.

CHAPTER 14

Minnie's Inn

Cooking was my mother's passion— not because she was a gourmet cook—but rather because she was dedicated to making basic food delicious. She believed in balanced and healthy meals long before that philosophy became main stream. Every supper consisted of a colorful plate of protein, salad, starch, and a vegetable followed by a delicious desert. Leftovers never went to waste since she was the casserole queen. Even when money was in short supply, we ate well. Mother's plan for supper began early in the day. She served fresh vegetables or the previous summer's frozen or canned supply at every meal. Venison from my father's hunting trips was served at least twice a week. In addition to stewed, baked, and fried venison, we ate a lot of fish and chicken, but beef was a rarity. From age ten, I was expected to help buy groceries, cook, and clean up. During warm weather, I pulled my red wagon to downtown Webster to the food market. In the winter my sled was piled high with groceries. I tried to find all the items on my mother's list. One time I came home with a cabbage instead of a head of lettuce; and I was never sure if the butcher wrapped up the right meat. Budget shopping and money management were skills I learned at an early age.

My mother's pies and cakes were always in demand for church fund raisers and by family members and friends. One year she received ten advance orders for her chocolate mocha cake to sell at the church bake sale. I cut and wrapped cardboard trays for the sheet cakes, helped frost the tops, and sprinkled them with nuts. My mother's nickname was Minnie, and on one of his trips to Webster, Jack Miller created a sign for our back door that said "Minnie's Inn." Had her health been better, she could have run Minnie's Bed & Breakfast.

My mother was the mistress of the spoon and spatula, but my father was the master of the hammer and screwdriver. He could build anything and was often called on by others to do so. My father knew math better than most high school graduates and could design cabinets and room renovations with skill. Much of our income came from Dad's remodeling and building jobs. He was so precise and detailed in his work that it took a great deal of patience to be around him when he was remodeling someone's space. Everything had to be perfect or he made it so. His colorful language would have made a sailor blush when he made a mistake or couldn't figure something out. "Fred's Fix It Shop" would have been a good sign to hang on the back door under "Minnie's Inn."

CHAPTER 15

Small Town Fun

*I*n the early 1950s television was growing in popularity. My family finally managed to buy a small black and white set. I loved to watch *The Lone Ranger*, the variety shows with Milton Berle and Perry Como, *Sky King*, and *I Love Lucy*. *Gunsmoke* aired in 1955, and my father and I never missed an episode.

However, my favorite kind of entertainment involved playing with the other kids in the neighborhood. We had the freedom to play our made-up games for hours on end without parental supervision. One summer my neighborhood playmates and I sat on the street curb and wrote down license plate numbers for hours on end. Points were awarded for every tag listed, with bonus points being added for out-of-state tags. I earned the most points by filling dozens of pages in a spiral notebook with useless numbers. During the hot summer days, we sold Kool-Aid on the curb and in the evenings after the traffic and the heat died down, played Kick the Can and Red Rover in the street. In fall we raked leaves into giant piles for jumping and arranged the leaves to make walls for a pretend house. My friends and I dragged our dolls and doll furniture outside to play with in the leaf house. Snow forts in the winter and snowball battles with the boys against the girls kept us warm when the weather turned bitter cold.

The spring I turned ten, eight of us kids were playing touch ball in the neighbor's back yard. I was pushed too hard from behind, and I fell forward crushing my right arm. My elbow was shattered, and I was in a lot of pain. Our doctor recommended to my parents a relatively new orthopedic surgery to repair my elbow with the use of steel pins. Without the surgery, the doctor said I would never be able to straighten my right arm. We had no health insurance and no money to pay for the operation. Our neighbors filed a liability insurance claim, since the accident occurred on their property, and the doctor willingly did the surgery with no payment up front. Two surgeries later, I regained the full use of my arm and didn't have the crooked arm we feared. My right arm was in a cast for weeks on end, and for the last two months of fourth grade, I wrote with my left hand.

Webster's annual Fireman's Carnival was the much anticipated event of the summer. Every July the large field to the west of town sprouted tents, booths, and carnival rides. Large trucks filled with erector set girders, carousel horses, bumper cars, and assorted wheels and motors were emptied and the equipment assembled for the much anticipated week of fun. The village of Webster threw its support behind the effort since the annual budget of the volunteer fire department depended on it. Firemen from the neighboring villages participated in the kick-off parade that traveled down Main Street and on to the carnival grounds. Local high school bands swayed to the marching music, fire trucks blasted their sirens, beauty queens waved gloved hands from convertibles, and politicians with red faces sweated their way along the parade route. When the police motorcycle contingent passed by, the carnival was officially open.

I earned my carnival spending money by doing chores around the house or for the neighbors, such as feeding pets, watering plants, and buying groceries. As I got older I baby sat, took in ironing, and cut grass. I carefully planned how I would spend my money, dividing my hard-earned quarters between riding the Ferris wheel, the merry-go-round, and bumper cars. The remainder went to cotton candy, funnel cakes, and numerous games of skill in the hope of winning a stuffed animal or carnival dish to take home. Starting in seventh grade, my parents allowed me to meet girlfriends and boyfriends on the midway for an evening of innocent fun. Occasionally, I rode with a boy to the top of the Ferris wheel where we could see all the way to Lake Ontario. That was a highlight of my summer, guaranteeing lots of bragging rights when I returned to school in the fall.

CHAPTER 16

A Christmas to Remember

*M*y Christmas memories in Webster are very vivid. Even though our family continually struggled to make ends meet, somehow Christmas was always bountiful, and peace prevailed at least for a while. How my parents did it I will never know; but I think my Mother squirreled away money each week all year to have extra for Christmas.

With the cold wind and snow blowing in across Lake Ontario during December and the dry heat in our apartment, Mother was usually confined to her bed. It was my job to help buy the food and last minute gifts for our holiday celebration. Several days before Christmas, I bundled up like Nanuk of the North and braved the snowy banks and slippery walks to purchase the last remaining items on Mother's shopping list. My journey began with a trip to the drug store for a prescription, the grocery store for bread, and finally the Candy Kitchen where my senses engaged the minute I walked in. Every homemade confection imaginable was arrayed in the glass cabinet–sugar glazed nuts, chocolate Santa's, crunchy peanut pillows, and crispy rainbow colored strips of ribbon candy. After buying one-half pound of each and some fudge for Pop, I chose a delicacy to nibble during the walk home.

Starting at Thanksgiving, I thumbed through the Montgomery Ward catalog making dog ears on pages that displayed items on my wish list, hoping there would be some of them under the Christmas tree. One year I talked constantly about the school set I found in the catalog–teacher plan books, a pointer, and report cards. I must have read the description a hundred times. When Christmas morning came, it appeared there was no school set from Santa Claus, and as I opened each gift my heart sank. Finally, hidden in the back of the tree, the last gift I opened was the school set. From that day forward, I taught school until I wore out all my friends, neighbors, and stuffed animals.

Other Christmas gifts I remember during those years were my growling brown bear—all three of us sisters got one. Lay him down and his eyes closed; bend him over and he growled. A huge white stuffed dog, a two-story doll house with lots of furniture, and a beautiful walking doll with moving legs were extra special gifts I received.

Janice and Audrey provided a great surprise for me one Christmas by giving me a pink and gray record player and a stack of "45s." Other gifts that year included gray Bermuda shorts with a buckle on the back, a pink shirt, and knee socks, which were the style then. At school during lunch hour, my classmates and I were allowed to play records and dance. Glenn Miller's "Moonlight Serenade" or Marty Robins "White Sport Coat and a Pink Carnation" were favorite dance songs.

One year when I no longer believed in Santa Claus, I sensed that Christmas was not going to be the same. Dad and I drove to a local farmer's lot to choose the best tree we could afford. Back at our apartment my father's patience and language were put to the test as he attached the stand, then dragged the bulky tree up two flights of stairs into the living room. It was my job to decorate the short needle fir with big multicolored lights, shiny glass balls, and lots of shimmering silver icicles. That tree, like our family, had seen better days. My parents' persistent poor health and financial problems cast a shadow over our festivities that year.

Freezing weather outside meant the old oil furnace in the basement worked overtime. Since we lived upstairs and heat rises, we stayed plenty warm, but the dry parched air made my mother's asthma much worse, and the Christmas tree didn't like it either. My bedroom was next to the living room and at night when the house was still, I listened to the drip, drip, drip of needles bouncing on the floor. They became a steady shower as the days wore on.

It wasn't unusual for a real tree to lose needles, but that year there were more than the normal amount to be swept up. By Christmas Eve, our tree was on life support. A steady rain of needles turned into a downpour and glass ornaments crashed on the floor. On Christmas morning a tree skeleton stood in our living room. The unopened gifts were covered in brown fir needles and shards of glass over one inch thick.

In northern New York in the 1950s, European Christmas traditions prevailed. That meant the tree went up one week before Christmas and stayed up for twelve days until January 6 of the New Year. All opened gifts remained displayed under the tree to be admired and shown to everyone who dropped by. The excitement of un-wrapping my long-awaited gifts didn't overcome the cloud of sadness that engulfed me that Christmas day. I was crying by the time the last present was opened. Our naked tree just wouldn't do, since I couldn't show off my tree and gifts to my friends.

I cried and carried on so that my father agreed to go look for a new tree. After breakfast, he drove the old car around town until we saw several trees at a roadside stand. The farmer saw us coming and met us at the barn door probably wondering about folks who go looking for a Christmas tree on Christmas day. It was my job to explain why we were there and that we only had five dollars to spend on a tree. "No charge!" the farmer said, as he loaded the tree into the trunk of our car. Once again my father sputtered and fumed as he attached the tree stand and dragged the new tree into our apartment. I didn't dare complain as I spent the rest of that Christmas day stringing lights, hanging decorations, and cleaning up piles of dead needles.

Even though I have many memories of other Christmas days, that one always comes to mind. I think it's because I learned an important lesson from my experience with that lifeless Christmas tree that would serve me well later in life. My father helped me find the new tree, and the generous farmer provided the gift, but it I had to use my ingenuity and hard work to save the day.

Frieda-age 12, The "moose" deer head

CHAPTER 17

An Unexpected Event

*A*n unexpected event occurred when I hit the impressionable age of thirteen that affected the remainder of my life. Memories are fickle. Things probably were never as good as you remember or never as bad, but certain events leave an indelible impression like a water mark on your personality.

We were all sitting at the dining room table after eating one of my mother's delicious meals when my fifty-three year old father stood up to his full six feet and suddenly crumpled to the floor. The shock of seeing him lying there and the mad rush to get help from the neighbors is still fresh in my memory today. My strong, feisty father was carried down the stairs on a stretcher, and I didn't know if I would ever see him again. I packed up my clothes and moved next door for an extended stay with the neighbors.

Our family life would never be the same after Dad's cerebral hemorrhage or stroke. My father's surgery to strip the bulging varicose veins in his legs had most likely been the cause of the stroke. It sent a blood clot to his brain. A promising job in Rochester and the necessity of passing the company physical had made the surgery a requirement.

He spent the next two months in the hospital trying to recover the use of his legs and hands and learning to talk all over again. My mother seldom left his side. Needless to say, he never got the promising job, and our family entered a new era of hardship.

Our family finances were stretched to the breaking point since Dad was unable to do any work for almost two years. Mother took as many odd jobs as she could find, from substitute teaching, to long term babysitting, to cooking for friends and neighbors. When she stayed busy and productive, her bouts with asthma were less severe.

I baby sat and ironed to earn as much money as possible. Fellow church members, neighbors, and the Webster Community Chest benevolence fund helped out wherever they could. That first Christmas after Dad's stroke, they made sure there were gifts and goodies for every member of the family. Dad regained most of his motor skills, but his speech was slurred and affected the rest of his life. That was a cause of great frustration for him. When he was finally able to go back to work, the only job he could find was as a janitor. It was my job to help him clean our church and our town hall office buildings. I could earn five dollars on a Saturday, which I saved for my school expenses.

In September before my father's stroke, my sister Janice eloped. After working in Rochester for two years, Jan had gone to New York City to train to be an airline stewardess. While working for Eastern Airlines, she met and married Curtis Whaley, an Eastern pilot from Georgia. My parents were very unhappy about the elopement. Once Mother adjusted to the news, all she dreamed about was moving the family to Georgia where we, too, could make a fresh start. I was just beginning high school, and the thought of moving and leaving my life in Webster filled me with apprehension and anxiety. At that time, I had no idea that indeed my years in Webster were numbered, and I would spend the greater portion of my life in Georgia.

The next June after my father's stroke, Audrey married her high school sweetheart George Kimmel. There was a lot of tension leading up to that wedding. It was difficult for my parents, who were still adjusting to my father's illness and recovery process, to deal with another daughter's wedding plans. Audrey worked long hours to pay for the wedding and bought the fabric for my hand-sewn bridesmaid dress. It was very hard on me to have both of my sisters leave the Webster area just when I was beginning my teenage years.

CHAPTER 18

High School Sororities

Upon starting high school, I had four goals. I wanted to become a member of the Library Club, French Club, Debate Club, and a sorority sister. Webster was very class conscious and the social sororities were at the center of things. The sororities were not sponsored by the school, but served to organize the girls in Webster for social activities and community service. All the girls in town worried about getting into the right colored sorority. Every sorority had its color cardigan that was a badge of honor to wear. Green and White was for the socially-connected crowd. If you lived on Lake Road or Bay Road, it meant that your father had a good job and your parents had money, which made you a shoe-in for the Green and White. The Blue and White sorority was reserved for the smartest girls who were in the Library Club.

I had top grades and had already been accepted into the Library Club, so I expected to wear a Blue and White sweater like Audrey had when she was in high school. During sorority rush week, I wrote letters to the sorority sisters in several different groups requesting admittance. After an agonizing two weeks, the invitations were passed out. I didn't receive even one invitation—and to put it mildly—I was crushed. My mother told me to "get over it" and eventually I did; but it left a scar. During my sophomore year, I was invited to join the Black and White sorority. That group of girls turned out to be a lot of fun, and I gained many wonderful friends. During sorority initiation, new members were required to do silly stunts. I had to sneak into my neighbors' garages and gather up clothespins. Then I clipped them on the fir trees in their yards. The next morning, I had to return to the scene of the crimes, clean up the messes, and apologize for my mischief, as I returned the clothespins to the rightful owners.

Hard times always teach us lessons we might never learn otherwise. My father's stroke and my feelings of rejection as a teenager were tough at the time, but I learned that rejection was a part of life. It made me more sensitive to others in my school that were different, or poor, and often ignored by others. I decided I would never try to make anyone feel inferior or unimportant or judge someone based on what their father did for a living.

CHAPTER 19

Cheer Up Pop

My parents' strong personalities continued to be my predominant influence during my teenage years. I constantly walked on eggshells trying not to upset either of them. My father mellowed somewhat after his stroke but suffered from chronic depression. Mother often told me to do something to "Cheer up Pop!" I tried with limited success, but deep down was afraid of my father's temper that easily boiled over. He often became frustrated when he couldn't form his words clearly or do a task as well as before his stroke. Amazingly, he could swear with perfect clarity. The only time Dad was truly happy was when he was with his brothers and life-long friends at their Adirondack camp during the hunting and fishing seasons.

My mother didn't have Dad's quick temper, but she was very emotional and cried about everything. She ran the house and the people in it. She determined how the household money was spent and who would do what and when. She was also a fixer—someone who was always trying to fix somebody else. It was very difficult for me to talk to her about anything personal. I wished we could have been more open and honest with each other.

Any questions about sex were strictly off limits and triggered an avalanche of tears. My mother falsely believed little Fifi Minnow could do no wrong, and I strived to not disappoint her or my father. On rare occasions when I got into a bit of mischief, I knew better than tell my parents and face the consequences.

Every night for supper our menu included a dose of history, world events, and politics, as well as a good meal. Some of our discussions were very heated, especially during an election year. I was expected to share my parents' political opinion that all Democratic politicians, especially FDR and Truman, were good and all Republican politicians, like Eisenhower, were bad. My parents believed that only unions looked out for the common man and were always right; whereas big business, particularly banking and insurance companies were greedy and took advantage of the ordinary person. As a member of the school debate team, there were many opportunities for me to use the arguing skills I learned around the family dinner table.

In the Library Club, School Council, and French and Debate Clubs, I always took on leadership roles. I wore myself out helping to plan club events, sock hops, and pep rallies. Debate Club gave me confidence and poise and the ability to speak to large groups of people. A lot of times, my health suffered in the process, and I got headaches, stomach aches, colds, and allergies. I was driven to achieve, which was a blessing as well as a curse. Part of it was my attempt to overcome my feelings of inferiority. If I worked hard enough and well enough, people noticed and complimented my efforts.

I threw myself into my studies and other extracurricular activities at school and at church. My favorite subjects were Social Studies, History, English, and French. Science and Math were more challenging for me, and I struggled with those classes all through high school. My high school chemistry teacher, Miss Tuttle, lived downstairs from our apartment. The door to her efficiency unit was always open to me. She helped me with my math and science homework and provided a listening ear for me when I was dealing with my parent's issues upstairs or when I wanted to talk about boys. She became a substitute big sister as we bonded in her tiny kitchen while mixing up Chef Boyardee pizzas for supper.

As a teenager, I chafed with having responsibility for my parents' mental and physical well-being. I wanted to be more carefree and be allowed to dream big dreams. In my school, girls were encouraged to think about what they wanted to do with their lives. Most females at that time worked as secretaries, teachers, or nurses. I still liked the idea of becoming a teacher but also dreamed of being an interpreter at the United Nations and traveling the world. I fantasized about romance, marriage, and having my own family one day, and how I would do things differently when I had the chance.

CHAPTER 20

Girlfriends and Boyfriends

Two of my best girlfriends in Webster were Halley Hafner and Trudy Strauss. Halley and I were school mates from the third grade on. She and I had become friends during elementary school when we had joined Girl Scouts. We had bonded at Scout day camp while we made paper mache` bowls and boondoggle braided necklaces. As Scouts, we did our patriotic duty every Memorial Day and marched a mile to the veteran's cemetery to decorate the graves. The year my broken elbow was in a cast, I still marched and placed my flowers on the graves of the war heroes. Three years in the Scouts, however, were enough for me. I liked earning merit badges, but Girl Scout camp was not something I enjoyed. My hay fever and asthma acted up when we slept in tents, and I was afraid to swim in Lake Ontario. Haley stayed in Girl Scouts longer, and we drifted apart until the seventh grade.

Trudy moved from Canada to Webster before Halley and I started high school. She was born in Germany and fit right in with the many other kids of German descent. Trudy was an "out-of- townie" and lived close to Halley. We became a best friends' threesome. My friends' mothers decided that all proper young ladies should learn entertaining skills and etiquette. We three joined the Tea Party Club that met monthly at a member's house. Each month we were taught a different homemaking or hostess skill. Halley's mom taught us how to knit mittens, another mom taught the art of making fudge, and another how to properly serve tea. We always dressed up for those special events, white gloves and all.

When we entered high school, Halley, Trudy, and I joined different social sororities, but our friendship bypassed that color-coding system. The three of us were involved in extracurricular activities and intramural sports, with the two of them being much more athletic than I was. Everyone in high school was required to take gym class and wear awful green gym suits. I really stood out like a sore thumb because instead of buying a new green suit, I had to wear my sister's awful hand-me-down blue suit.

Hosting or attending a pajama party was a much anticipated event. A sleepover at Trudy's house turned into an unintended adventure. Put a gang of teenage girls together, and we could usually think of a way to get involved in mischief. One of the neighborhood boys invited all the girls at the PJ party to come over after dark to his pool for a swim. He said he wasn't going to be there, but it would be fine for us to use the pool. We tried our best to be quiet as we snuck out of Trudy's house and walked down the street past Halley's house heading to the pool. Most of us didn't have bathing suits, and we wore what we had. Others were skinny dipping. We did our best to be quiet and whisper, but one of the girls let out a scream as someone pushed her into the water. Suddenly, flood lights lit up and we were caught. There was a lot of ranting, raving, and apologies to be made once all our parents found out.

The Webster Teen Canteen was my favorite place to go on Saturday night. My girlfriends and I went in a group hoping to find dance partners for the jitterbug, the twist, the bunny hop, and the fox trot. The top forty hit tunes sung by Johnny Mathis, Connie Frances, Pat Boone, Elvis Presley, and others were my favorites. It was great fun for me to use up all that energy on the dance floor and temporarily forget about the problems at home.

The popular girls in school never lacked for attention from the boys I secretly admired. I felt insecure and unable to measure up to the cute petite type that boys favored. My French nose and protruding teeth were too prominent for anyone to call me cute. In my mind, I was a female version of a nerd. A lot of my clothes were homemade or altered hand-me-downs. I wanted pretty clothes like all the other girls. My family did their best to help, but it was usually up to me to earn money to buy clothes for the sock hops and other events at school. I poured through the Montgomery Ward catalog looking for stylish clothes that I could afford. In spite of my best efforts, the clothes on those dog-eared pages never looked as good on me as they did on the models in the catalog.

I usually had a boyfriend, but not the type I was hoping to attract. The needy underachievers in school with relationship issues were the ones who liked me. Two of those boys lived for sports—basketball, football, and track. Since I made good grades, I helped them with their homework and sympathized with their problems at home. I think they were looking for a girl who was more a mother than a girlfriend. In spite of our differences, I was always glad to have a date for school dances and sports events. Since I lived close to the high school, I could walk to all the basketball games. One night I brought three members of the team back to our apartment because the weather turned stormy and they didn't have transportation back home. Mother refused to wake my father to ask him to drive. Instead, she supplied the boys with blankets and pillows and told them they could sleep in the downstairs hall. We really heard it from the landlord the next day.

My idea of a perfect boyfriend was someone who succeeded in school and had ambition for his future. My senior year I dated a boy the same age but one grade behind me, who met all my criteria. However, he was definitely in the relationship for fun and was not as serious about me as I was about him.

Whenever a boy brought me home after an event at school, my mother went on high alert. While my date and I sat on the front porch talking and snuggling, Mother flipped the porch light off and on. During cold weather, while I stood at the bottom of the stairs

61

leading to our apartment hoping for a goodnight kiss, she repeatedly flipped the hall switch until I came up the stairs. The 1950s were a more innocent time for relationships between the sexes, and most boys behaved themselves. I knew the ground rules for dating and did not like my mother snooping on my activities. I felt she didn't trust me to act like a lady. Her strictness became easier to understand after I was informed of her history and learned about my half-brother Jack.

CHAPTER 21

Expanding My Horizons

*I*t's said that travel broadens you and expands your horizons. Two trips I took during high school to visit my sisters made that kind of impact on my life. Sending a thirteen-year-old girl alone on a train from Rochester to New York City would be frowned upon today. But for me in the late 1950s, it was an adventure of a lifetime. My married middle sister, Audrey, was living on Long Island while her husband, George, was in army basic training at Ft. Dix, New Jersey. When the train landed at Grand Central Station, I was dumped into a sea of humanity with no sign of my sister. We finally found each other and spent the next several days riding the subways to experience all the sights and sounds of the Big Apple. That was my first real experience with big city life, and I loved the hustle and bustle of it all.

The trip home proved to be another kind of adventure. A good looking college guy, probably attracted by my mature appearance, sat by me and talked about his studies at Rochester Institute of Technology. We laughed and talked all the way to Rochester, but I never told him I was not yet 14 years old. He phoned me after my return to Webster and asked if he could come see me. My parents agreed to let him come for a visit. After they met him and realized how old he was, they made me tell him the truth about my age—a very embarrassing experience.

By my junior year in high school, my dreams of going to college were diminishing. My Yankee work ethic and ambition led me to believe that I could do anything; but I was discouraged from following those dreams because of our economic circumstances. I know, however, my parents did the best they could to make sure I always had what I needed or wanted. Mother often sacrificed to provide money for school activities and made sure I always had nice birthday and Christmas gifts. But I was baffled that my college-educated mother didn't see the need for me to further my education, nor to help me explore options for scholarships and financial aid.

"What does Frieda do after graduation?" was frequently discussed by adults in the room without much input from me. Everyone weighed in—my sisters, my aunts, my grandmother, our neighbors, our church minister, and my parents. I wanted to go to a New York State teachers' college with brick buildings and a beautiful campus, but I was told that there would be no money for clothes or extracurricular activities, let alone tuition. And since all those things were important to me, too, I realized that my dream would not come true.

My oldest sister Jan and her husband Curt came to my rescue. My brother-in-law was a Southerner, and my sister and their children had easily adapted to the Southern way of life. They offered to let me live with them in Atlanta, Georgia, where Curt was based as a pilot for Eastern Airlines. They would help me go to school, but I would not have the luxury of a four-year teacher's education. Instead, I was expected to go to secretarial school to learn skills for a job. During the summer after my junior year, I boarded an Eastern DC-3 in Rochester and headed south to discover a new way of life—Southern style.

The low, slow flight down the East coast to Atlanta revealed higher mountains than I had ever seen and a gradual change of dirt from black, to brown, and finally to the red clay of Georgia. Extreme heat and humidity, air conditioning, sweet tea, barbeque, Johnny Reb's Dixieland, beautiful Buckhead mansions, and the radio theme song from *Gone with the Wind* are my lasting impressions of that trip. Jan and I visited Massy Business College in downtown Atlanta, where I was enrolled in the Starr Executive Secretarial Course and Finishing School. The plan was in place and my path was set, but I had to finish high school before my new venture could begin.

CHAPTER 22

Senior Year

My senior year at Webster High School was the most memorable of my years in school. I was a serious-minded girl, but during my last year of high school, I decided to have a bit more fun. I served in leadership positions in clubs, worked on the school yearbook staff, and had a role in the Senior Play, *Life with Father*. I cheered on our basketball and football teams as they won state championships. I campaigned for John F. Kennedy, helped to conduct our high school's mock election, and was thrilled when he became President. My boyfriend and I attended the senior prom and all the other dances and parties during the year. Audrey took me shopping in Rochester and helped me select the perfect dress for the prom—a vision of blue and white loveliness.

I was driven to make good grades, pass the New York State regents exams with all A's, and managed to graduate second in my class. That special year came to a close on a hot, sultry night in the school gymnasium, as I stood in my white and gold gown and delivered my Salutatory speech to my classmates. Little did I realize how quickly my life was about to change.

I was oblivious to how unhappy my parents were about my impending departure for Georgia. My grandmother Schryer had died in the fall of 1960, and my father hadn't been the same since. My mother tried on many occasions to talk me out of moving to Georgia after high school. Looking back now, I realize my parents had serious issues and I served as a buffer between them. Neither of them wanted to deal with what we call empty nest syndrome. Because I didn't want to leave my boyfriend behind, I could have been easily convinced to stay in Webster. I was surprised however, to find out that my boyfriend's family permitted his dating me only because they knew I was leaving soon for Georgia. His future would involve out-of-state college and not the excess baggage of a girlfriend.

In spite of my mother's objections and my reservations, Jan and Curt insisted on my move to Atlanta. I was already enrolled in secretarial school and for at least six months would be learning some marketable skills. However, my parents hoped that at the end of my studies I would return to Webster to look for a job in Rochester. A significant chapter of my life came to a close in July 1961. With apprehension as well as excitement, I was eager to discover what new opportunities were waiting for me in Georgia.

Senior Year–age 17

PART TWO

"Trust in the Lord with all your heart, and lean not on your own understanding. In all your ways acknowledge Him, and He will make your paths straight" (Proverbs 3:5-6).

CHAPTER 23

Red Maples to Red Dirt

*I*n 1961 Atlanta, Georgia was in transition. The city was struggling to bridge the gap between the old South and the new. Racial problems dominated the Atlanta headlines, with battle lines drawn between those who were segregationists and those who believed in integration of the races. Water fountains and restrooms for colored people and so called "separate but equal" colored schools were a prominent part of the Georgia landscape. It was a restless city trying to decide whether to remain a small center of commercial activity or grow into an urban metropolis.

The building of the interstate highway system opened up new opportunities for development northwest of the city, and with the perimeter highway under construction, all portions of the suburbs were soon accessible. My sister's house was at the end of a long driveway on Moore's Mill Road. A sunken train track ran next to the house, and day and night loud freight and passenger trains barreled out of Atlanta heading to points north. There was hope that the train bed would become a part of a new light rail system and that the Whaley's property would be purchased for a station. But the light rail proposal that would allow a free flow of traffic to the northern suburbs was soundly defeated.

With my high school diploma barely dry, I boarded a flight taking me from my home on the flatland of Lake Ontario to the red hills of north Georgia. In 1961 flying was a unique and special event that required me to dress up, wear heels and hose with straight seams, and be on my best behavior. I sat in the window seat and watched as the dark brown dirt and red maples of New York State faded into the distance. After two plane changes, the red dirt, tall pines, and fragrant magnolia trees of north Georgia once again came into view. As the plane descended, I said goodbye to my childhood and the life I had known for the past seventeen years. Ready or not, I was transported into young adulthood as I walked down the steps of the plane at Hartsfield Airport and into the hot, humid air of a typical July in Georgia. I realized there would be no turning back. Only on rare occasions would I again enjoy the cooling lake effect summer breezes in the small town of Webster that had been my home. I was greeted by Jan and whisked to my new home north of Atlanta where I started the next phase of my life as a member of the Whaley household.

When I moved to Georgia after high school, I had no idea what my future would hold. Many challenges and blessings were on the horizon, but I couldn't see that far ahead. But God in His providence saw the big picture and moved me out of my comfort zone to a place ripe with new experiences and new influences. The southern "Bible Belt" culture would have a profound impact on my life. I didn't know it at the time, but I was desperately in need of a lifeline to help me navigate the difficult days ahead.

CHAPTER 24

Culture Shock

*I*t was one thing to visit Atlanta during the previous summer; it was another to permanently plant my feet on southern soil. My Yankee accent stood out like a sore thumb, and it soon became apparent that I didn't have a clue about how to talk. Back in New York, we took pride in the proper pronunciation of English, and people in my family took the Lord's name in vain with great abandon. Neither was acceptable in the South.

"Yes ma'am" and "no sir" replaced "Yup," "Yes," and "No." All my properly pronounced "ing" verbs were abbreviated to "goin," "callin," "doin," and my very favorite, "fixin to." That fizzy drink known as "pop" became "co-cola" and the hot liquid I steeped in a pot and drank black was now loaded with sugar, ice, and lemon.

There is an old saying in the South: "I might have born a Yankee, but I got here as fast as I could." In other words, Southerners considered their lifestyle so compelling that even Yankees couldn't wait to plant their feet in the South. I'm sure it was true for some, but I was homesick and missed the Webster way of life. I struggled to adjust to the muggy heat and missed the cool lake-effect breezes back home. My boyfriend, senior year accolades, and friendships soon became memories, and instead of being the big fish in the little pond, I reverted to my early childhood nickname of "Fifi Minnow"—little fish in a great big pond.

It didn't help that my parents were not happy about my move to Georgia to live with Jan and her family. My mother, in particular, was very lonesome. She worried about me constantly. Every phone call and letter made me feel guilty about having left my parents to fend for themselves back in Webster. They didn't make a good adjustment to having an empty nest. They also had to find another way to deal with the household responsibilities I had assumed at home.

There is some truth about the birth order of siblings. Jan and I fit the stereotype perfectly. We had been separated by distance and had grown apart as sisters. I didn't realize how dominating her personality had become. As the first born, she was always in charge and treated me like the baby of the family. I probably was spoiled and didn't like her acting as my mother. My parents were called upon to be the mediators of our disputes. The battle between North and South took up where it left off one hundred years earlier. One of the biggest ongoing arguments concerned whether my parents should move south, too. Mother wanted to; Dad didn't; Jan wanted them to; I just wanted everyone to make up their minds and quit "fussin" about it.

CHAPTER 25

Back to School

Money and the lack thereof was always an issue for me. My brother-in-law, Curt, co-signed a loan for my secretarial courses, which would take me six months to complete. We had to dress professionally for school each day, so I used my high school graduation money to buy shoes and fabric, which Jan and I sewed into skirts and dresses. While finalizing my admission at Massey Business College, Jan and I heard about a girl from south Georgia who was enrolled in the school, and living in her car. Jan was also a person with a big heart who had taken in one stray, so she offered to let Frances move in the guest room with me. Frances and I shared a room off and on for the next three years. Frances was a more fun-loving person than I was and often served as a buffer between me and Jan when our relationship was tense.

Walking was not an option in suburban Atlanta. The sidewalks and quiet streets in Burke and Webster were replaced by busy four-lane highways. Nevertheless, every school day, I walked downhill in my skirt, hose, and heels to the Greyhound bus stop about one quarter of a mile away. After a long hot ride into Atlanta, I walked uphill to Massey Business College and reversed the process every afternoon.

It would be six months before I would get my first car. My high school driving class along with Dad's frustrating attempt to teach me to drive, had left me intimidated by traffic instead of road worthy. So in the meantime, I invested my remaining money in driving lessons and learned to drive the Whaley's large station wagon.

The Starr Secretarial Course at Massey Business College was a new venture and greater challenge than I expected. Math, English, and Letter Writing were a cinch after my tough high school curriculum. But typing and office machines involved mechanical skills I didn't have. In order to move to advanced typing, I needed to pass three timed tests—sixty words per minute with no more than three errors. Typing was the one class I had to take twice. The finishing school classes were the most fun—grooming, wardrobe style, and personal presentation. The easiest part for me was public speaking because of my debating experience.

There was no shortage of new experiences and new people. Frances was always finding cute guys for us to double date. And I managed to meet some nice college students in the Peachtree Road Methodist Church College and Career Class. That group loved field trips and retreats, and we were always planning for the next weekend retreat or trip. I helped organize the food and Bible studies for our frequent camping expeditions to Stone Mountain.

Every letter or phone call I received from my parents, Mother in particular, made me feel guilty for having left them in Webster. They were also insistent that I return to live with them after graduation and find a job in Rochester. After four months of school, I returned to Webster for Christmas to visit my parents. During that trip, my boyfriend and I realized that our relationship could not survive the distance. With his leaving for college in June, it was time for both of us to move on. It was not easy for my parents to accept that I liked my new freedom in Georgia and would not be moving back to New York. But I had charted a new path and wanted to see where it would lead.

CHAPTER 26

Romance Southern Style

*A*fter graduating from Massey Business College in the spring of 1962, I started my first secretarial job with a small company that built pre-fabricated houses. A new company, Colonial Pipeline Company, hired me six months later. Colonial, with its headquarters in Atlanta, was building a huge pipeline from Texas to New Jersey. It was a great place to work in a corporate environment and provided me the potential for advancement. I started out in the finance department as a secretary to three of the managers. The men wore suits and ties, and the female dress code required skirts, dresses, hose, and heels. I really felt quite grown up when Curt helped me buy a small black Ford car. I had a paycheck and my own mobility. It was quite a change in my life in less than a year.

I was barely eighteen years old and working with people a lot older. My rather sheltered upbringing often left me feeling anxious and insecure. An underlying pessimism and negativity about life in general robbed me of a lot of joy. Most of the people in the office drank and partied, and since I didn't do either, at times it was hard to fit in. Jan and Frances were just the opposite and they constantly chided me to relax, party, and not be so serious about everything. But one night, when I decided to throw caution to the wind and stayed out past my midnight curfew with some other singles from church, Jan and Curt pitched a fit. And rightly so; I did have an obligation to let them know where I was.

By the fall of 1962 I decided to go back to school and enrolled in Georgia State College in downtown Atlanta. Earning a college degree had always been one of my priorities, but I didn't realize how hard it would be. My New York State education trained me to be very interested in public service, so I chose a major in Political Science. Being a college student and full-time employee taxed me to my limit. When I wasn't at work or in night school, I was doing homework, so my social life was severely curtailed.

Lured by the glamour of public service and politics, I resigned my job at Colonial Pipeline and decided to work in the Georgia governor's race. It didn't take me long to realize I'd made a serious mistake. Even though my candidate won, I ended up in a steno pool at the state Capitol. That was not where I wanted to be. After three months of misery, I was reinstated as a secretary at Colonial Pipeline in the construction engineering department.

At Colonial Pipeline there was no shortage of single men. For a while I dated a man who was more interested in me than I was in him. One day by the elevator, he introduced me to his friend and co-worker, Talmadge Davis. In some ways Talmadge reminded me of my boyfriend from Webster, only older and more mature. Talmadge invited me out after I broke things off with his friend. On our first date, we went to see the movie, "The Days of Wine and Roses" with Jack Lemmon and Shirley McLain. We hit it off so well, we started dating on a regular basis. He was tall, wore a crew cut, and had a dry sense of humor. It didn't bother me that he was a chain smoker—many of my family members smoked—or that he was almost seven years older than I was. Since I was the serious type, it was nice to date someone older who was more serious, too.

Jan liked him, but for some reason she didn't think he was right for me. She knew that I had a lot of ambition, and she didn't sense that in Talmadge. He worked as a clerk in the engineering department coordinating all the purchase orders for the pipeline construction. I was impressed that he was a graduate of the University of Alabama, had a good job, a nice car, and treated me like a lady. Like most big sisters, Jan thought she knew what was best for me, and she wanted me to date other men. The ones she picked for me were definitely not my type. I wanted to get away from all the family pressures, and dating Talmadge gave me that opportunity. We soon realized we were in love and wanted to have a future together.

Talamadge's home town of Ragland, Alabama was located about thirty miles northeast of Birmingham. We drove to Alabama so I could meet his mother and other family members. After that trip, we began talking about a serious commitment, engagement, and marriage. In the fall of 1963, we flew to Webster so he could meet my parents. Talmadge joked to my family and friends that he was a great-grandson of Jefferson Davis, President of the Confederacy. His southern twang probably convinced some people he was telling the truth. My parents were not enthusiastic about Talmadge becoming their future son-in-law. For them, it meant that I was taking one more permanent step away from home. Mother even tried to contact my former boyfriend to encourage him to start seeing me again.

Upon our return to Atlanta, we announced our engagement at Colonial Pipeline, knowing they didn't allow married couples to work in the same department. I applied for and received a position in the legal department at Colonial, and in spite of my family's lackluster support, I started making wedding plans.

The tug of war between my parents, my sister, and me got so bad that I moved into an apartment with Frances and her friends in an attempt to get away from all the stress. That decision proved to be a big mistake. Frances and her friends liked to party, and there were always boys spending the night in our apartment, which I couldn't handle. Talmadge and I moved our wedding date from April to January to try to escape the mounting pressure.

Everything seemed to go wrong in the week leading up to the big event. A huge snowstorm shut down the city of Atlanta on January 10.

My five-year-old nephew developed mumps and had to be quarantined for a week. Talmadge was exposed, and we were all on pins on needles waiting to see if he would get sick. Mumps was not a good thing for a grown man to get. My parents balked at coming for the wedding, but finally relented, and when the Atlanta airport reopened after the snowstorm, flew in on the Thursday before the ceremony.

On January 18, 1964, I marched down the aisle at Peachtree Road Methodist Church on my father's arm wearing a lace, ecru suit with matching shoes and a fur pill box hat with a small veil. Jan was my matron of honor, and Talmadge's high school buddy from Ragland, Alabama his best man. An outside observer might have thought it was my funeral with Mother crying all during the chapel ceremony and the small reception at Jan's house. My mother was an emotional person, and it was difficult to see her last daughter married off.

After a weeklong trip to Gatlinburg for our honeymoon, we settled down to married life in a one bedroom apartment close to Lenox Square in Atlanta. After being surrounded by so many people for so long, we liked having our own space. We had friends and family over to eat and hosted a wedding reception for Frances and her new husband, Larry. I found that I really enjoyed being a new bride and keeping house. I poured myself into my marriage, cooking, and decorating. I couldn't settle for less than perfection. My expectations were very unrealistic, since I wanted everything to be like it was portrayed in *Good Housekeeping* magazine.

CHAPTER 27

A Dose of Reality

The construction phase of the pipeline project and the need for Talmadge's work at Colonial's Atlanta office was winding down by the summer of 1964. He received a short-term assignment for a project in Macon, Georgia and moved there taking our only car. Every weekend during that summer, I rode the hot Greyhound bus from Atlanta to Macon. The bus stopped at every railroad track and cattle crossing on the route making me motion sick by the time Talmadge picked me up at the bus stop in Macon. At the end of the summer, Colonial Pipeline transitioned from construction to operations. The construction employees were given the opportunity to bid on a field position somewhere along the pipeline route. Talmadge was assigned as an operator at Colonial's new pumping station in Pelham about twenty miles south of Birmingham. In October of 1964, we packed up our belongings, left our first apartment, and headed to Alabama.

A towering iron statue of the Roman god Vulcan, the god of fire and forge, stood at the top of Red Mountain looking over the city of Birmingham, Alabama. Vulcan was cast from local iron forged in the iron ore and steel mills of this industrial city nicknamed the "Pittsburgh of the South." Birmingham in 1964 was ground zero for the clash between the civil rights protestors, led by Dr. Martin Luther King, and the states' rights enforcers, led by Gov. George Wallace and Police Chief Bull Connor. We arrived in Birmingham the year after the racially motivated tragic bombing in Birmingham that had killed four little girls attending Sunday school at the 16th Street Baptist Church.

A small apartment complex close to downtown became our first residence, as we acclimated to our new locale. Our unit was on the second floor sandwiched between loud feet over us and loud music under us. The thin walls didn't mute the arguing on one side of our bedroom or the crying baby on the other side. Talmadge was glad to be back in his home state, closer to his mother and the influence of his alma mater, the University of Alabama. For me, it was a huge adjustment to find my place as an outsider in the really Deep South.

Talmadge swapped his office job in Atlanta for a Birmingham field job working rotating shifts. That meant five day shifts, two days off; five evening shifts, two days off; and five night shifts, followed by one long weekend off each month. The other off days came in the middle of the week and constantly changed. One top of that, the pumping station ran on "pipeline time" meaning there was no change to Daylight Savings Time. Operations ran 24/7/365 including holidays. It was a constant battle for Talmadge to sleep during the day and for me to get good quality sleep with no routine. His body's biological clock stayed totally out of sync with the demands of the job. It was hard for both of us to keep up with when he would work, what time he had to be there, and when he would be off.

This brutal schedule took a toll on our marriage. We lived in a small apartment where we met some other couples, but it was difficult for us to plan any social activities because of his work. He worked most holidays, making it hard to attend family gatherings back in Ragland. I longed for routine with a husband who left for work in the morning Monday through Friday, came home for dinner, and had weekends off. I had given up a job I really liked at Colonial's headquarters in Atlanta. Being a new bride and wife in a strange city with no car and with a husband always at work or asleep was not my idea of a happy marriage. He was tired and testy, and I was irritable and unhappy with our life. Since it seemed unlikely that I could change my circumstances, I started searching for answers that would enable me to cope.

CHAPTER 28

Spiritual Birth

*E*ven as a young child, I was aware of God's power and presence in the world. I enjoyed going to church and all the activities and events that were offered for children and youth. My relationship to God, however, was based on me being morally right so that He would love me. Since I had a very high standard of moral behavior for myself, I found it easy to judge other people and their behavior. My parents loved me and did their very best to show that love to me, but for some reason, I always felt their love was conditional and based on my behavior. I looked at God in the same light.

During my childhood, most people considered me industrious, ambitious, honest, studious, moral, friendly, and empathetic. These were virtues I chose to live by, but my understanding of God and my Christian faith were still mostly intellectual—of the head and not the heart. I also struggled with the darker side of my personality. Chronic depression kept me from seeing the positive and upbeat side of life. I longed to find unconditional love and was disappointed when my relationships fell short. I wanted to be happy and at peace but felt that my home life conspired against me. I emerged from childhood a pessimist, worry wart, and a "fixer" who never seemed to be satisfied with life.

As I approached my twenty-first birthday, I struggled to find a way to cope with my new circumstances and overcome the depression that had settled on me like a dark cloud. My life had not turned out the way I had expected, and I looked for something that would fill the void in my life. Since I had yet to make a real friend in the Birmingham area, there was no one in whom I could confide the deep longings of my heart.

When we were living in Atlanta, I had tried to convince Talmadge to go with me to the Methodist Church where we had been married. He said he would not attend such a liberal church. He had been raised Southern Baptist but had been inactive in church since he had left home. On one visit to his home in Ragland, we attended the local Baptist Church with his mother. The preaching was loud and full of hell fire and damnation. I said I would never be a Southern Baptist, so we were at a spiritual standoff.

With nothing else to do and no direction to follow, I started studying with the Jehovah's Witness and Mormon missionaries who came by the apartment. In addition, radio preachers offered up all sorts of promises from groups I'd never heard of before. "Just send in your money," they declared. "You will receive healing and a blessing." I ordered Bible studies from the radio preachers and read books written by religious philosophers who were more uncertain about the truth of the Bible and the meaning of life than I was.

In the mid-1960s, the "God is Dead" movement was in full bloom which caused great theological debates between seminary professors and traditional church leaders. The more I listened to the debates and studied and read about the controversy, the more confused and miserable I became. I know it was at the Holy Spirit's urging that I began to read through the New Testament to try to sort things out in my mind. In reading the Gospels, I became reacquainted with the Jesus I had learned about as a child in Sunday School. I remembered the Bible stories depicted on the stained glass windows in my childhood Methodist churches in Burke and Webster. I thought of the loving compassionate

Jesus—the gentle Shepherd who watched over his flock. I so wanted to believe that God was not dead and that the Bible was not just a book of irrelevant stories.

On March 15, 1965, I fell on my knees by our bed and in despair and tears told God that if He was real to let me know it. His great compassion, forgiveness, and love flooded my heart. I asked Jesus to change my life and give me a purpose for living. At that moment my life was transformed by the His saving power. My tears dried up, and I felt a peace in my soul that I had never experienced before. I realized that God had always loved me unconditionally and was able to forgive all my sin and shortcomings. Even though I knew the circumstances of my life would not change, I felt hope that God would help me handle those circumstances. It slowly began to dawn on me that God had a plan and purpose for my life that he would reveal to me one step at a time. I didn't understand it at the time, but God's gift to me was a spiritual lifeline that would hold me and that I could cling to in the darkest days to come.

I wanted to tell everybody, especially my family, what had happened to me. Talmadge was glad that I was feeling better, but he didn't really understand what I had experienced. Jan let me know right off that she didn't think much of my beliefs and that Karl Marx said, "Religion was the opiate of the masses." Audrey listened but brought up all the latest intellectual arguments against Christianity—to which I had no response. I didn't have all the answers, but I knew that I was no longer depressed and that I could handle life once again.

I had no idea where to start looking for a church. Once again Talmadge said, "I will not go to a Methodist church, but if you can find a Southern Baptist church, I will go with you." In upstate New York, Southern Baptists had been considered "holy rollers," so I had to overcome my bias and at least give that church another try. The local yellow pages listed many Baptist churches, and I drove around seeing where each one was located. Our first visit was to Raleigh Avenue Baptist Church. After attending several services, I began to understand what it meant to have a personal relationship with God through His Son

Jesus Christ. I recognized that was what had happened to me as I knelt by my bed. I acted on my faith and requested baptism by immersion and church membership. Talmadge transferred his membership, and my new life as a Christian Baptist began.

When I shared my newfound faith and desire for believer's baptism with my mother, she said, "You were baptized as a baby and sprinkled when you were twelve and that was enough for anybody." I immediately began praying for my family members, asking God to help them find their way to a true relationship with Him.

CHAPTER 29

Political Fever

Talmadge and I started house hunting in the Birmingham suburbs. Mrs. Davis generously gave us sufficient down payment for a small two bedroom ranch in Homewood, an older suburb on the southwest side of the city near our new church. We were also able to buy a used second car which was a big help. Now I could drive and go shopping and regain some measure of control over my life.

With a house payment and two car payments, I decided to look for a job to help with the family finances. It was also important for my mental health to stay busy. My legal experience in Atlanta helped me land a position as a legal secretary at Bradley, Arant, Rose & White, the top law firm in Birmingham. With me away from the house during the day, it was easier for Talmadge to sleep and prepare for his evening and night shifts at Colonial Pipeline. He and I were like two ships passing in the night. We didn't see much of each other except on his one long weekend each month. So it was good for me to stay busy doing productive work with interesting people. I enjoyed dressing professionally every day and having lunch with the other secretaries at the office.

Early in 1966 my boss, John Grenier, announced his resignation from the law firm and threw his hat in the ring to run as a Republican for the U.S. Senate from Alabama. Since I was still a political junkie, I decided to switch from Democrat to Republican after I was asked to work in the Grenier campaign office. What I thought would be a stimulating job didn't turn out that way at all. I found myself stuck at headquarters answering phones on the weekends, going to cocktail parties that I didn't enjoy, and putting out political signs during the hot Alabama summer. Talmadge did not like the crowd I was associating with. It probably didn't help that they were Republicans and at that time most Alabamians, including Talmadge's family, were fervent Democrats. Many still held a grudge against Republican President Lincoln who had freed the slaves, given them the right to vote, and ordered Union troops to invade the South. Lurleen Wallace, the wife of Governor George Wallace the arch segregationist, was running for governor, and the states' rights, anti-segregation rhetoric was intense.

I was suspect since I was born a Yankee and had more liberal ideas than Talmadge's family and friends. I didn't really understand the depth of feelings and emotions on both sides of the racial issue. I leaned toward integration but also saw firsthand the problems that came with merging the schools and churches. Civil disobedience was hard to see in a positive light. I often found myself in the midst of heated debates when people talked so ugly about integration. It was not easy to be attacked for expressing my opinion.

Grenier lost the November election to Democrat Senator John Sparkman. It would be many years before Alabama became a predominantly Republican state and John Grenier helped to make it happen. After losing the election, he decided not to return to the law firm, but devoted the remainder of his life to politics. I was asked to come back and work for one of the other attorneys, but I declined since Talmadge and I decided it was time for us to start a family.

CHAPTER 30

Motherhood

As the months dragged on with no baby in sight, I tried to stay busy. I couldn't take on enough jobs in the church. It looked like I was still trying to work my way to salvation. I worked in Vacation Bible School, volunteered in the church office, taught GA's (Girls in Action), and for a while Talmadge and I taught a children's Church Training class. I think I felt that if I did enough and worked hard enough, God would somehow find me more acceptable to Him, and my family would find out how much my life had changed. As a new Christian, I still didn't understand the fullness of God's grace and power. I was soon to learn those lessons and many more.

Stuart George Davis was born on February 7, 1968, one day before my twenty-fourth birthday. I'd had an uneventful pregnancy, but as the weeks dragged on, I didn't think he would ever get here. I was huge and two weeks over my due date when the doctor decided to induce labor. It was a good thing, because that 10 lb. 2 oz. boy needed to come out. George Davis was his paternal grandfather and Stuart sounded like a good strong name to go with it. Talmadge was so proud of his big boy and showed him to everyone who visited the hospital nursery. "That's my son hanging out of his basinet," he bragged. After five days in the hospital post-partum, I was ready to go home. I hadn't slept in the noisy hospital and hoped at home I could better adjust to nursing our new son. Mrs. Davis came to stay for a week after his birth and helped my transition to motherhood.

Stuart was a colicky baby, which was a family trait on my side. Because of his size, he was hungry all the time and definitely not inclined to sleep. Every time Stuart coughed or cried, I went into high alert. He woke up with colic around 3:00 a.m. and stayed awake for hours at a time until he was soothed enough to be put back into his crib. In the early morning darkness, I cried and prayed, asking God to help me be a good mother. That lasted long after the typical three months for a baby to settle into a schedule. I was on the verge of post-partum depression.

With Talmadge's irregular work hours, I had no sleep routine. I had always been a light sleeper, easily awakened as a child by my father when he was rattling around in the kitchen at 5:00 am every morning. Now Talmadge kept me awake when he came in from the evening shift. Older mothers told me to sleep when Stuart slept, but I never could sleep during the day. Young mothers at church seemed to adapt to all the demands of a new baby. Since I struggled, I felt sure there was something wrong with me.

God knew just what I needed—a friend, another new mother who was struggling with parenthood just like I was. Shirley Bobo entered my life at just the right time. My Stuart and her Danny were toddlers. We shared our Christian faith and mutual struggle to raise our strong-willed boys. Her husband was usually working, drilling with the army reserve, or hunting. Shirley was always willing to listen and offer compassionate practical advice for whatever was going on in my life. It helped that she had a great sense of humor and was more optimistic about life in general than I was at the time. We soon were babysitting each other's boys and taking them on shopping trips and other excursions. We both liked to sew, mainly to save money, and shop for fabric. More than once she came to my rescue when I just couldn't take it anymore.

After his first birthday, Stuart started having colds, ear infections, itching skin, and wheezing. Whenever the weather turned cold and damp, the wheezing turned into croup. The pediatrician and allergist diagnosed rhinitis, asthma, and eczema—the triple play of allergy miseries. Life became much more complicated when allergy tests revealed all the air borne triggers he would need to avoid to stay healthy. I stripped his room of all curtains, stuffed animals, and rugs on the floor. The walls, windows, and floors were frequently washed, and everything with perfume or odors was thrown away. Multiple food allergies were also identified, and I had to make drastic changes in the kitchen. Dairy, eggs, nuts, chocolate, and several other common foods had to be avoided. I started making his bread and most other foods from scratch with no preservatives.

All my efforts helped somewhat, but my son still spent way too much time sick and taking medicine. He could no longer go to a friend's house if they had a dog or cat, and I had to take his food to church events or preschool. We had good health insurance, but the co-pays and other expenses really added up. Talmadge refused to believe that his smoking in the house made Stuart's asthma worse, and that caused friction.

Allergies ran in my family. I had suffered with hay fever and asthma growing up and old musty books or moldy smelling basements put me over the edge. I never could camp out in a tent or cabin without getting sick. My mother had asthma her whole life, and it seemed unfair that I had to live with it again. I wouldn't say I was mad at God about it, but I surely did have a lot of questions. I felt responsible for Stuart's poor health, since all his conditions ran in my side of the family.

CHAPTER 31

⌒

Snow Birds

*M*y parents decided to leave Webster after it became obvious I was not returning to the family nest. Jan and Curt convinced Mom and Dad to move south, so that Dad could supervise the construction of the Whaley's new house in Newnan, Georgia. Jan and Curt rented a small brick ranch for Mom and Dad to live in and helped with all the logistics of their move.

During my high school years, my mother had talked frequently about relocating to Georgia, but after moving to the South, all she talked about was moving back up North. She didn't like the heat or humidity and hated air conditioning, and my father wanted to be close to his hunting buddies.

Having my parents in Georgia made it easier for me and my sisters to spend time with them and not have to travel so far for a visit. I was living in Alabama, Audrey in Louisiana, and Jan in Georgia and we didn't have to fly into upstate New York to see our parents. None of us were happy when less than a year after their move to Georgia, my parents packed up their things and headed back to Webster. Two years after that they moved back to Burke where I was born. As far as my sisters and I were concerned, it was not a good decision. The cost of heating their drafty dwelling in that long, cold, northern New York climate was very expensive, and we knew they couldn't afford it.

To resolve that issue, my parents decided to become "snow birds." Every fall before the first snow, Mom and Dad packed their station wagon and headed back to Dixie. They stayed at each of their daughters' houses for several weeks at a time before heading back north in the spring. My life was further complicated when they spent six to eight weeks at my house sometime during the winter. My father took on many fix-it projects around the house, and my mother assumed many cooking duties, but three generations in our little house did not work very well.

Between Talmadge's irregular work and sleep schedule, Stuart's chronic allergies, and my parents' bickering, I stayed in a constant state of anxiety. I felt like it was my job to keep everyone happy and the house quiet so Talmadge could sleep. We enjoyed having a built-in baby sitter at first, but as the visit dragged on, Talmadge wanted to know when they were going to leave. He kept up that drumbeat the whole time Mom and Dad were there. His mother was a very independent person and he didn't understand why my parents were so dependent on their children. He did not appreciate my mother's continual humming and unsolicited advice about our marriage, his job, and Stuart's allergies.

CHAPTER 32

A Second Son

I was finally adjusting to the demands of my life, and Stuart was just becoming more independent when I found out I was pregnant again. I prayed hard for a healthy baby, free of allergies, and secretly wished for a girl. Instead, Michael Schryer Davis was born on September 25, 1971. He definitely was not premature at 9 lbs. 4 oz. and definitely not a girl. But we were thrilled to have another son and Stuart a little brother. Even with his healthy size, Michael spent his first few days in an incubator with respiratory problems. I decided not to nurse the second time around and made a better adjustment to motherhood since I was getting better sleep. It didn't last long. Before his first birthday, Michael's body was afflicted with terrible allergies and eczema.

Both Stuart and Michael developed the itchy, blistering type of eczema behind their knees, in their elbow crooks, and on their hands and feet. Stuart's feet stayed so broken out his socks stayed bloody most of the time. By the time Michael was walking, he was in the same situation. Creams or lotions didn't help, and the side effects from taking so much medication were worse than the cure. Michael was diagnosed with food allergies with some similarities to Stuart, but with enough differences that they couldn't eat the same things. Both boys ended up getting tonsillectomies and that helped their frequent strep throats. Several days each week, I was at the pediatrician and allergist offices trying to stay on top of the latest flare up of croup or asthma.

My heart broke for the boys and all their medical problems, and there was nothing I could do about it. I knew it frustrated Talmadge to see his sons suffering so much. And it didn't help that the medical bills kept coming in with no end in sight. Talmadge was usually working when the boys got sick, so their care was primarily my responsibility. I was exhausted and worn out and depressed most of the time. My faith was tested to the max as I fervently prayed for God to make them well.

Audrey was an important member of my support system. Talmadge and I had visited her home in New Orleans before the boys were born. During that time, I had shared with her the change that a personal relationship with Jesus had brought to my life. At first Audrey was skeptical, but she listened intently to my testimony. A seed was planted in her heart and it grew after she met some other dynamic Christian ladies in the New Orleans area. Audrey, too, became a born-again Christian, and her life changed dramatically. I was thrilled to know that my physical sister had also become my sister in Christ. Now there were two of us to pray for the rest of our family.

Audrey's family frequently moved due to George's climb up the corporate ladder. They were living in Houston, Texas when I reached the end of my cope. She and George offered to pay for airplane tickets for me and the boys so come visit them in Texas. Talmadge wasn't too pleased with the idea, but I jumped at the opportunity. That trip proved to be a life-changing event.

During that visit, I realized that Audrey's faith had grown and surpassed mine. Her example helped me realize I was once again trying to change my circumstances instead of trusting God with them. I saw my role as a wife, mother, and daughter as a burden to bear instead as an opportunity to grow in the Lord. After much prayer during that trip, I realized the sovereign hand of God was at work in my life. Prior to that time, I was mad at God for not taking away my problems. Now I saw that God once again wanted to change me in the midst of my problems. As I left Houston, I had a renewed assurance that even though my circumstances might not change, God would strengthen me to deal with whatever I had to face.

The boys and I flew home with Michael screaming all the way because of an ear infection and changes in cabin pressure. Normally, I would have been a basket case, but instead I had a calm serenity that God was in charge and that He would see us through. That assumption would be tested even more in the days that followed.

CHAPTER 33

On the Move

After Michael was born, Talmadge considered finding other employment. Neither of us thought his grueling schedule was good for his health or our family. After a long job search, he accepted a position in management training with Southern Bell, the Birmingham phone company. His regular hours and weekends off were a welcome relief. After two months, much to my great dismay, he quit the phone company and reapplied for his old job at Colonial Pipeline.

Talmadge's main goal was financial security and he felt he would have more of that with Colonial. He felt a great responsibility to take care of our family financially. That was important to me as well, but I wanted us to live a normal life with room for church, recreation, and friends. It was only God's grace that prevailed and allowed me to get through that difficult time.

The eight years we lived in Alabama were a plus for our family. Stuart and Michael were born there, we bought our first house, I trusted my life to the Lord, and began growing in my Christian faith. In 1973 a better job with Colonial Pipeline in the Atlanta, Georgia area was put up for bid. Talmadge won the bid, and soon we sold our house and prepared to move. It still meant the same chaotic, rotating work schedule, but I was excited to be moving back to Georgia. I would be closer to Jan and her family in Newman, and I had always liked the Atlanta area. And the timing was perfect, since it was summer and Stuart was starting kindergarten in September.

My friend, Shirley, and I vowed to keep our friendship alive despite the distance between Birmingham and Atlanta. The Davis' family roots were deep in the Alabama soil, but there was no opportunity for Talmadge to advance with his job by remaining in Alabama. The small stub pipeline that ran south of Birmingham had already been scheduled for automation. With an opportunity to get a better paying job in Georgia, he decided to go, but he was never happy with his decision.

CHAPTER 34

Georgia on My Mind

*I*f you asked a local for directions in getting around Marietta, he told you to hang a left or a right at the "Big Chicken." And you would have already identified yourself as being from somewhere else if you said "Mary-etta" instead of "May-retta." The Big Chicken was a fifty-six-foot tall tower built to look like a chicken on the top of Johnny Reb's Chick, Chuck, & Steak at the intersection of the "four lane" at the intersection of Hwy. 41 and Roswell Road. This advertising billboard was also used as a navigation landmark for small light aircraft landing at the local airport and military planes landing at Dobbins Air Force Base and the Lockheed Georgia Aeronautics Company.

The Marietta Square housed the courthouse and various Cobb County government offices. In 1973 Marietta and unincorporated Cobb were considered great places to live and raise a family. The schools were the best in Georgia, and Atlanta was far enough away that urbanization, traffic, and crime were not big issues. It was there that we decided to begin the next phase of our lives. I was excited that the boys were entering their school years and that it would be easier on me for them to be out of the house and more independent.

While Talmadge worked, Jan and I conducted an exhaustive house search in Cobb County northwest of Atlanta. Our limited budget would buy only so much square footage, but we finally found a fixer upper with a big yard in Marietta. The house was larger than our previous one in Birmingham, with more space and a second bathroom. Some things about the house were not to my taste, such as the bright red carpet throughout and a chewed up window in the basement where the previous owners' parrot had lived. But Talmadge liked to do yard work and enjoyed fix-it projects. Since the house was a split level, the upstairs bedroom provided more seclusion for his daytime sleep. A good tree cover kept the master bedroom cool and darker than the rest of the house.

Stuart started kindergarten, and I enrolled Michael in a mothers' morning out program. The enjoyment of those peaceful mornings did not last long. As soon as fall began, the boys' allergies flared up and got worse than they had been in Birmingham. We put both boys in one room so I only had one bedroom to keep stripped and sanitized. I diligently prepared their different diets so that most meals looked like a cafeteria line with different foods on each plate. I had a fleeting thought that I might go back to work part time to help with medical expenses, but between Talmadge's work schedule and the boys' illnesses, the idea was unrealistic.

When they weren't sick, Stuart and Michael were imaginative, creative, high energy boys. They were limited in outdoor activities during the cold weather months, but when weather and their health permitted, they loved to build forts in the woods with their friends and ride their big wheels down the hills on Favorwood Drive.

They liked to read and pretend they were pirates, cowboys, and soldiers. Their large collections of Lego blocks, space toys, and games and puzzles were constantly strewn throughout the house. Trying to keep them quiet when their father was asleep was no easy task. Sibling rivalry was rampant when Michael got into Stuart's stuff. I was a pretty strict disciplinarian and often overreacted to some things I should have ignored.

They both did well in school with Stuart usually at the top of his class. Michael struggled to make good grades because of his allergies and the effects of his medication. In second grade, he missed so many days with asthma I wondered if he would be promoted to third grade. Early in life, both Stuart and Michael developed the ability to rise above adversity and accomplish their goals in spite of how bad they felt.

Their birthdays and Christmas were always celebrated in a big way. I learned how to make egg-free cakes and cookies so the boys wouldn't feel left out. I started shopping weeks ahead of time to make sure they received the gifts on their wish lists. I made homemade Halloween costumes and school play outfits and bargain hunted for their clothes, shoes, and toys so they could enjoy the same things their friends had. When time and the boys' health permitted, Talmadge took them rock hunting and fishing, which were two of his favorite hobbies. It provided good bonding opportunities between father and sons.

During the winter of 1975, a massive snow and ice storm blanketed the northern part of Georgia. The snow was two to three feet deep on top of a layer of ice. Our house sat at the bottom of a hill and at the back of a large yard with underground springs. As the temperature plunged, the water coming out of the faucet slowed to a trickle and finally stopped all together. Our electricity stayed on, but we had no water for eight days. The neighbors next door were unaffected by frozen water pipes. We ran our garden hose to their outside faucet and kept a trickle running all the time so that we had water to boil for cooking and for flushing toilets. After eight days, our front yard was still buried in snow and ice while the road ice was finally melting. The novelty of building snowmen had come to an end, and we all had a bad case of cabin fever. As I was looking out our big bay window praying for relief, a massive brown geyser suddenly erupted in the front yard. The ruptured water meter spewed muddy water for at least three days until it was determined whether the break was on our side of the meter or the street side. Unfortunately, we ended up having to pay for the repairs and the massive cleanup.

CHAPTER 35

❦

Storm Clouds

We joined a nearby Baptist church and involved the boys in age-appropriate activities. Vacation Bible School was the biggest event of the summer, which I always taught and the boys attended for two consecutive weeks. I was also involved in our Women's Missionary Union activities and prayer retreats, taught a ladies' Bible study, and was at the church every time the doors opened. Church was a place where I could excel and use my organizational skills to accomplish some good. Many days there was little I could accomplish at home with Talmadge asleep, so the church became my safe escape and a place where I could make a worthwhile contribution.

Libby Garrison was another young mother who attended the same church and was husbandless on Sundays like I was. It was very difficult for both of us to get our children to church and then sit alone surrounded by couples and families. A common bond was formed between us that strengthened us in our determination to raise our children to be Christians regardless of our husbands' availability or participation. It helped that our four sons were close in age and enjoyed playing together.

Our friendship withstood many difficult circumstances and tests over the years.

Our most memorable family vacation took place in 1975, the year before the Independence Day Bicentennial. We took a trip up the east coast, visiting Luray Caverns, Gettysburg Battlefield, Mount Vernon, and Monticello. We then drove through New York State to Burke to see my parents. We took the boys to High Falls for a picnic and let them splash in the refreshing water. I felt like I had passed on a family heirloom to my sons.

Because of his experience in the initial construction of the pipeline, Talmadge was given an assignment in Spartanburg, South Carolina during the summer of 1977. I packed up the boys, and we moved into his apartment for two almost normal months. The boys swam in the apartment pool and played with their new friends. We enjoyed the company of a family from Switzerland. Even though Talmadge worked six and seven days most weeks, we still had our evenings together, and I didn't want that relaxing, stress-free summer to end.

Once we were back in Marietta, my parents continued their annual winter visits. Talmadge was still not happy about their long stays, and I stayed constantly frustrated trying to keep peace and civility in the household. I wanted the boys to love and respect their grandparents, but I wanted my parents to respect my household and marriage. My older sisters and I didn't always agree on what any of us could or should do about it. Whenever my parents returned North, Talmadge and I argued about what should be done before the next year. I wanted us to sit down and have a rational conversation with my parents telling them that the most our house and finances could handle was a two-week visit. He believed it was my responsibility alone to confront my parents, which I was not emotionally prepared to do.

My parent's health problems persisted, and my mother's asthma and bronchial complications usually required a doctor's visit when my parents were at our house. My father never fully recovered from his stroke and had limited communication skills. The boys' allergies kept them feeling bad most of the time. They had dark shadows under the eyes and usually kept a runny nose and cough along with dry, itchy, bleeding skin. No matter what any of us did or the doctors recommended, their problems persisted. I was always bone tired and easily got viruses and infections. Talmadge stayed run down because of his lack of sleep, and we passed things from one to another.

One Christmas day when the boys were young, we all had the flu. Talmadge held Stuart, and I rocked Michael and we waited for two days until we felt well enough to open our gifts. I had many female problems and continual PMS, which resulted in me having a hysterectomy when I was thirty-three years old. Although I successfully recuperated from the surgery, I stayed fatigued and overwhelming tired all the time. It was easy to blame my ailments on being overworked and overstressed.

None of us were prepared when my father was diagnosed with esophageal cancer when he was seventy-one years old. Dad had always been a smoker and had graduated from cigarettes and a pipe to cigars and chewing tobacco. Since their move back to the rural town of Burke, the closest hospital was in Plattsburg, NY. My mother never learned to drive a car and Dad was too weak to drive the long distance for tests and radiation. Relatives and neighbors drove them to my father's appointments. With my sisters and me all living in the South, it was very difficult for us to help our parents during that time. Jan and Audrey flew up as many times as they could to help. My options were more limited by finances and the young age of my boys. The radiation kept Dad from eating enough to keep his big frame nourished. He looked emaciated, and it became apparent he was losing his battle with cancer. But even with their health problems, my parents continued to drive south each year for the winter.

CHAPTER 36

An Unwelcome Diagnosis

*I*t was inevitable that things would reach a crisis point. In May 1980 I came down with the flu of all flues. I was in bed with a high fever, chills, and miserable aches and pains. It was one week before the big wedding that was planned for my niece, Sandy Whaley. The wedding was to be held at her fiancé's church in Atlanta with the bridesmaids' luncheon planned for my house on the big day. Mom and Dad stayed longer than usual into June to be here for the special event, and it was my responsibility to get all of us across Atlanta to the rehearsal dinner and ceremony. Talmadge was responsible for keeping the boys entertained.

I crawled out of bed to attend the rehearsal dinner and put finishing touches on plans for the bridesmaids' luncheon. Mother was a big help in the kitchen preparing much of the food. We had made everything from scratch and, fortunately, a lot of it was already in the freezer. My parents left for New York after the weekend of wedding festivities, and I fell into an exhausted heap.

I had already committed to teaching two weeks of Vacation Bible School, and I was determined to go to Ridgecrest Baptist Conference Center for a week of Sunday school training. I had accepted the position of Sunday School Director at our church but decided that I needed training to be more effective at my job. Mrs. Davis agreed to drive over from Ragland to keep the boys, and I headed off with some other like-minded people from the Atlanta Baptist Association to Ridgecrest, North Carolina. The training week was challenging and a refreshing change of pace, but once I returned home, I knew something was seriously wrong with my health.

I itched constantly and was so fatigued it was an effort to get through each day. With our family history of allergies and eczema, I was convinced I had developed a food or medication allergy. And I was sure my fatigue was due to remnants of the flu and the demands of a much too stressful life. A visit to the boys' allergist for a complete workup didn't turn out as expected. My blood work labs came back with a surprising result. No significant allergies were found but my liver enzymes were elevated and the allergist recommended that I immediately see my regular doctor.

Thus began a two-year long ordeal to figure out what was wrong with my liver. I was referred to a gastroenterologist who started the testing process in order to make a diagnosis. None of the options looked good. The doctor pointed out the dangers of Hepatitis A, Hepatitis B, non-alcoholic fatty liver disease, and Hepatitis non A/B (now known as Hepatitis C.) He explained that the first three conditions were not desirable to get but could be treated. Hepatitis non A/B sometimes destroyed the liver, but he hoped that I didn't have PBC (Primary Biliary Cirrhosis) because it was always fatal.

My digestive system was poked, prodded, and peeked at from top to bottom with CT scans, MRI's, ultrasounds, and miniature cameras. I drank quarts of thick, gooey, bitter liquids and was punctured so often I felt like a sieve. I donated quantities of blood and other unmentionables to the hospital lab. The final step was the worst of all—a liver biopsy. Just a light sedation is all they allowed, as the giant hollow needle made its way through my rib cage into the liver. The pain and pressure was intense and it stayed that way for the eight hours I had to lie perfectly still following the procedure.

Based on the test results, my doctor began to eliminate the various forms of hepatitis, as well as the non-alcoholic fatty liver disease. Primary Biliary Cirrhosis was confirmed by the biopsy slide. The doctor explained that PBC is a rare liver-scaring disease that usually afflicts women in the prime of life. There is no known cause, but it probably is an autoimmune disease with a genetic component. The amount of time it takes for the disease to destroy the liver varies from person to person. It could happen very quickly or take as many as fifteen years. I was alone at the doctor's office when the bad news was delivered.

Driving home I felt a strange sense of relief that I finally had a diagnosis, accompanied by anxiety and the dread of how to tell my family and friends. The prevailing notion was that any person with cirrhosis must be a closet drinker or had abused their body in some way. Since I didn't drink alcohol, it was not going to be easy to explain my condition. Fortunately, I didn't have yellow eyes or skin and looked quite healthy. Only close friends knew how miserable I felt with all the itching and fatigue. It didn't seem believable to me, much less anyone else that I was a walking time bomb.

CHAPTER 37

A Change of Plans

*B*eing diagnosed with terminal liver disease at age thirty-seven was not in my life's plan. I'd only been married seventeen years, and Stuart and Michael were thirteen and ten respectively. I struggled with how to break the news to them. For years, Talmadge and I had tried to make sense of the boys' allergy problems. I had felt responsible for their allergies since all those miseries had come from my side of the genetic tree and here was another genetic-related disease I was imposing on my family. My fear that Talmadge would feel totally overwhelmed was justified. He felt so burdened by two sick boys, and now a terminally ill wife, that it fell to me to buoy everyone's spirits.

After telling Stuart and Michael the truth, we all had a good cry. They didn't really understand. None of us had any idea what we were living with, and in my case dying with. My parents were wrapped up in Dad's cancer treatments, and since nobody in either family had ever heard of this strange disease, there wasn't a lot of support coming my way. My mother did tell me that her mother, my grandmother, had died of some sort of liver disease in her early fifties, but in the 1930s everyone falsely assumed it was from alcohol consumption.

My belief in the sovereignty of God was severely tested. I couldn't help but ask, *God, why is this happening to me? Lord, I've given my life to you and have so much left I want to do for my family and for you.* Many times I felt like my prayers hit a glass ceiling. Intellectually, I knew God was with me, but I felt very alone. My friends Libby and Shirley were an outlet for me when I couldn't cope any longer. Every day was a struggle with some days better than others. One of my new medications helped to alleviate some of the itching, allowing me to sleep which resulted in an improved energy level. Shirley was in nursing school and had access to medical journals, but the articles she sent me describing the course of PBC were depressing. I reminded myself that no one knows the number of days God allows for each life, and that I should live each day to the fullest. I tried to carry on my life as normal as possible, which for me meant staying busy.

Every three months, I went back to the doctor for more blood work and, fortunately, my condition remained stable. During one of those visits, my doctor told me about PBC research at the Mayo Clinic in Rochester, Minnesota. Getting an appointment at the Mayo Clinic normally took months, but since he knew some of the researchers, he offered to make some contacts. Mayo set my appointment for the Friday before Memorial Day weekend in May 1982. Flying at the last minute on a holiday weekend was expensive, but Talmadge and I decided to take money from savings to make the trip.

My name had been on the LaBelle Heights Baptist Church prayer list for months. When our fellow church members heard about my appointment at the Mayo Clinic, they collected a love offering and presented it to us at the end of the worship service. It was enough to cover the two plane tickets, car rental, and help with motel costs. We felt overwhelmed by their love and generosity. Once again, Mrs. Davis kept the boys, and we headed for Minnesota with my liver biopsy packed in dry ice in my carry-on bag.

My initial consultation took two days, as I saw numerous doctors assigned to my case. In between clinic appointments, I worked on a piece of cross stitch needlework. The saying on that piece read *Teach me to feel another's woe and hide the faults I see. That mercy I to others show, that mercy show to me.* That was what I needed to be reminded of; others were experiencing equally difficult times, and I had a responsibility to pray for them. I made a point to get acquainted with others in the waiting areas of the clinic in order to share a word of encouragement.

While we waited for the test results, we decided to see as much of the area as possible. Everything in Minnesota was shut down for Memorial Day weekend, but we did find some interesting places to see. We drove into Wisconsin to the mouth of the Mississippi River past isolated farms that stretched to the horizon. The rich, black dirt and dairy farm silos reminded me of my childhood in upstate New York. The flat landscape was dotted with evergreen trees strategically placed to block the bitter winds that swept down from Canada. Patches of snow could still be seen in the distance.

My test results were delivered the Tuesday after Memorial Day with the same expected results. However, the doctors at Mayo were more encouraging about my long term prognosis. They prescribed some different medications and recommended dietary changes. It was good that Talmadge participated in all the consultations. We went away with a better understanding of what we were up against with this disease.

By nature and nurture, I am not an optimist. Much of my life was spent trying to overcome negative thinking about difficult circumstances. But after my trip to Mayo, I felt a sense of empowerment that with God's help, I would live for many years to come. God's still small voice comforted me and gave me hope that I would live long enough to see my sons to adulthood.

I wish I could say Talmadge felt equally encouraged, but that was not the case. It created some tension between us. He often asked, "How can you be so upbeat and positive about all of this?" I tried to explain to him about the peace and strength that God was giving me. He listened, but couldn't seem to find that inner assurance himself. I wanted us to live the days that we had left together as a family as fully as possible and was determined not to let his sense of impending doom defeat my upsurge in faith. But his tall, lanky body and thin shoulders felt weighted down by all the responsibility. In all fairness, he was the one bearing the burden for our mounting doctor expenses— along with the real possibility he would be left to raise the boys alone.

Michael, Stuart, Talmadge & Frieda 1986

CHAPTER 38

~

Good Bye Dad

Cancer claimed my father's life in March of 1983. When I saw him in January of that year in the hospital, I knew it was for the last time. He got his final wish to be in his house, his bed, and in Burke when he died. He lived twenty-five years after his stroke, and in spite of disappointments and setbacks, became more at peace with himself and the Lord. I was so thankful for the many early morning conversations we had about God and the importance of salvation through faith in Jesus Christ.

At his funeral we sang "How Great Thou Art" in the Burke Methodist church under the watchful eye of the saints of the Bible depicted in the colorful stained glass windows. Because of the frozen ground, Dad's burial had to be postponed until June. His final earthly resting place was on a rise with a view of his beloved rolling hills of the North Country, but I knew his eternal home was in heaven. During the service I read the following poem that I wrote for him on Father's Day in 1979.

To My Dad

As I thought about this Father's Day
approaching very fast,
I wanted to send to you a gift
that would always last.

So I decided I would write a poem
and try to tell my Dad,
The things about him that I love
that make my life so glad.

You taught me how to love God's world
and all the creatures that He made,
The birds, the squirrels, the rabbits,
the woods and meadows all arrayed.

You helped me with my school work,
especially my math.
And how needful it was to do my part,
and walk in an upright path.

Remember when you tried to
show me how to drive a car?
I have to say that was one time
you didn't get very far.

I was told by you to work hard,
and how to earn my pay.
Remember how we used to clean
the church each Saturday?

And then on many a Sunday when
we'd worship together at church,
That was where I learned of God,
for whom my heart did search.

And now that I'm grown up
and living on my own,
I can look around my house
and see the deeds you've sown.

My kitchen pantry, closet doors,
and very pretty flowers,
All remind me of the work you did
during many of your hours.

Our early morning conversations,
even though I am a grump,
Is one of the things I cherish
when I'm out of my a.m. slump.

It's thrilled my heart to share
my faith in Jesus with you,
And to see you want to read your Bible
and grow in your faith, too.

So on Father's Day I'll think of you
and all the things we've done.
I'll pray for you and send my love
from dawn 'till setting sun.

—Frieda Davis

CHAPTER 39

Planning for a Future

After my liver disease diagnosis, I didn't want to sit around and watch my days dwindle down. Two of my regrets were not finishing my college education and not keeping my skills fresh for the workplace. I had last worked as a secretary in 1967, but by 1984 computers had revolutionized office environments. I could type but knew nothing about DOS, word processing, and spreadsheets, so I considered going to technical school to upgrade my secretarial skills. My church work, especially in Sunday school leadership, brought back my childhood desire to be involved in education. For some time, I had felt that God was calling me to some field of church work. I was surprised to learn that the New Orleans Baptist Theological Seminary had opened a satellite branch in Marietta and offered an associate's degree in religious education.

One warm spring evening, Talmadge and I hiked the hills on Favorwood Drive and discussed the options for me to further my education. It meant sacrifices for all of us. The boys were old enough to stay by themselves for the few hours I would be in school when Talmadge was working. Mrs. Davis had invested money for each of us, so I could use my funds for whatever education I wanted to pursue. Talmadge didn't express an opinion one way or the other but urged me to follow my dreams. That walk set my course, and I enrolled in the fall semester at seminary.

It was not an easy path to choose. My goal was to become a Minister of Education in a Baptist church, which was not a common role for a woman in the 1980s. At Sunday school leadership conferences, I met a few women in religious education, but they mostly worked with preschoolers and children. I had no objection to preschool and children's work, but I felt called to work with adults as well.

The church we attended was small and had no staff other than the pastor, but he supported my interest, and the congregation voted to submit my required letter of recommendation to the seminary.

What was I doing? I wondered. *Few women went to seminary. I had a strange disease and now I wanted to do something strange with my life.* I was a New York Yankee in the heart of the Deep South, and my wishes and desires were different from many in my peer group. But my friend, Shirley, in Birmingham was back in school working for her RN, and another friend was considering law school. We used to joke that one day the three of us would open a clinic for women offering medical, legal, and spiritual advice.

Four other women enrolled in the religious education program at New Orleans Seminary extension in August 1984, but the five of us were a definite minority in all our classes. We were viewed with skepticism by some of the men in the pastoral studies program. However, the faculty went out of their way to make us feel welcome. I was in my element— back in school, studying the Bible, and learning how to organize and administer educational programs for the local church. I bought a used electric typewriter and began to pound out my class notes and papers. Never one to settle for anything less than an A, I studied hard for all the tests. When word got out about how well I did on my tests, class members wanted to meet with me for study groups. My meticulous class notes were in demand, and I soon realized that others were taking advantage of my diligence, so I began to charge two dollars a page for my notes. That money helped pay for my books for the duration of seminary.

Stuart and Michael seemed quite pleased that I was back in school and taking tests like they were. Talmadge seemed OK with my going to classes but didn't seem to like my time being taken up with homework. As usual, I made sure all the housework was done, food cooked, and all demands on my time were met. My fatigue and itching seemed to get better when I stayed busy doing something I enjoyed. Most people didn't know that I was dealing with a health crisis, since I tended to keep that information to myself and only revealed it on a need to know basis. I always was an ambitious person, and for some reason felt that I had to be accomplishing something significant to justify my presence in God's kingdom. It would have been easy to just give in to my disease and let the clock run down, but that was not who I was or wanted to be. My perfectionistic nature definitely was the reason for a lot of the stress in my life, but not the only reason.

CHAPTER 40

No Time to Say Goodbye

Talmadge's physical and mental health was of great concern to me. He smoked too much, drank way too much coffee, and wondered why he couldn't sleep. He stayed depressed much of the time, and his self-esteem was low. He took everything very personally and was short tempered with me and the boys.

Stuart was about to graduate from high school and go on to college. His dad convinced him to study something practical like engineering, so Stuart applied and was accepted at Georgia Tech in the electrical engineering program. Talmadge was not handling well the financial pressure of Stuart's college education, and I grew more and more concerned about my husband's state of mind as Stuart's high school graduation approached.

Talmadge's father was a smoker who had died from cancer at an early age. In my heart, I believed that's where Talmadge was headed. He finally agreed to see a doctor, who declared him in good physical health, but recommended that he take an anti-depressant and an anti-anxiety pill when needed.

We hosted a big graduation party for Stuart and both sides of the family were well represented. It was great to have so much family support. Stuart started on the Georgia Tech co-op program during the summer after high school graduation. He would work a quarter to help pay his expenses and then live on campus to study for a quarter. It would take him longer to graduate from Georgia Tech that way, but he would graduate with experience and fewer college loans. Michael had completed his high school freshman year and would soon be a rising sophomore. Our lives were definitely moving in a new direction.

Another change had taken place regarding our church life. Our small church had undergone a pastoral change, and the new pastor was not turning out to be what we had expected. During my tenure on the pastor search committee, we'd had the difficult task of replacing a much loved and well-respected pastor and his family. It would have been a challenge for any minister to fill the big shoes of our former pastor, but the new pastor the committee had chosen wasn't working out. His wife and rebellious son were causing all sorts of issues to erupt. As Sunday School Director, I was under a lot of stress trying to work with him. Talmadge refused to go to church anymore with all the turmoil going on. At seminary, I had taken two Bible survey classes from another local pastor, so we decided to try out his bigger church. Soon we joined that church and found it a place of solace where we could worship together as a family.

After Labor Day in 1986, Talmadge spent his off weekend with his mother in Ragland. He helped repair her house, worked in the yard, and threw some stuff away that she later dug out of the trash and put back in her house. I was hoping that those few days away from home would help him regain perspective. On September 14, he started his seven-day night shift at Colonial. Every morning that week I got the boys off to school, fixed him a good breakfast, and then we talked for an hour or so before he went upstairs to bed. He told me how much better he was feeling since starting on the anti-depressant, and we talked a lot about the boys and our future as empty nesters.

September 17, 1986 was a beautiful fall day in Marietta, Georgia. Talmadge was asleep, I was laying out cube steak to defrost in the kitchen, Stuart was at college, and Michael was in his room doing homework. Suddenly, I heard a loud thud, followed by Michael's scream. I raced up the stairs to find Talmadge lying beside our bed gasping for air. A pack of cigarettes had spilled from his shirt pocket. I threw the package of cigarettes into the bathroom and began pressing on Talmadge's chest screaming for Michael to get help from the neighbors. They quickly arrived from next door and called an ambulance. The paramedics continued the CPR and loaded my husband onto a stretcher and into the ambulance. I rode in the front of the ambulance to the closest hospital, where I sat waiting and praying. I called Libby and told her how to reach Stuart at his dorm at Tech. She arrived at the hospital just before I was called back to the family waiting room to hear the dreaded news, "Mrs. Davis, your husband died from a massive coronary." Nothing seemed real. Shock took over, and I was too numb to even cry. Even though I knew Talmadge's smoking and stress was harming his body, I expected it to be many years before I would have to say goodbye.

Instead, at age forty-two, after twenty-two years of marriage, I became a widow living with an incurable liver disease. I didn't really blame God, but I was totally mystified by it. In spite of it all, I didn't say "Why me?" Instead I tried to say "Why not me?"

CHAPTER 41

I Can Face Tomorrow

B y the time Libby drove me home from the emergency room, cars were parked all over my driveway and in the street. Neighbors and fellow church members descended on the house. Someone picked Stuart up at college and drove him home. He and Michael had to know something terrible had happened, but I asked people not to say anything to them except that their dad had suffered a heart attack. Once again my boys were going to hear life-altering news, and it was left to me to be the bearer of that news.

I took both boys upstairs and as calmly as I could, told them about their father's death. We were all sobbing by the time I was finished. After calming down somewhat, I felt compelled to say. "This is not God's fault and don't blame Him for your dad's death." I also told them I would do everything in my power to stay alive for them, but we would all have to work together to get through this difficult time. After talking to the boys, the full gravity of my loss settled in.

My niece, Sandy, was the first family member to arrive, and she took charge of everything until my sisters arrived from Florida where they both lived at the time. The police knocked on the door before dark.

Georgia law required them to investigate every death that occurred at home to make sure no foul play was involved. Their probing questions were an unwelcome intrusion.

My next challenge was how to tell Mrs. Davis about her only child's death. I couldn't just deliver the news over the phone. My plan was to call Mrs. Davis's sister to break the news to her first. I asked her sister to notify the Baptist minister and ask him to go with her to tell Talmadge's mother about his death. That was a good decision, since she would have people there to help her cope and plan how to get to Georgia. Then we had to contact Colonial Pipeline since Talmadge had been expected to work the night shift on the day of his death.

Nobody is ever prepared to make so many decisions amidst the turmoil of sudden death. Sandy stayed with me for two days and nights and helped me make funeral arrangements. My brother-in-law, Curt Whaley, drove me to Alabama to make arrangements for the burial. The ladies of Fortified Hills Baptist Church took over my kitchen and kept the food rolling in until the day of the funeral.

The packed memorial service was held at a local Marietta funeral home. The service focused on heaven as the destination for all who believe in Jesus Christ as their Savior and Lord. I had no doubt that was where Talmadge was at that very moment. We sang, "Because He Lives I Can Face Tomorrow." Those words helped comfort my aching heart.

Our friends from our former church, LaBelle Heights Baptist, drove our family to Alabama in their very comfortable motor home. After the graveside service, Ragland Baptist Church hosted a luncheon for everyone who attended the service. I was so thankful for so many who gave so much.

Jan and Curt stayed for a few more days and helped us celebrate Michael's fifteenth birthday. Everyone decided Michael needed a dog for a companion, so we all went to the Atlanta pound to find a puppy. I was too exhausted to fight and explain all the allergy-related issues a dog would bring to our household. Brownie became just one more responsibility for me to deal with. Audrey came after everyone else left to spend a week. She helped me clean out Talmadge's clothes and personal items and provided much needed emotional support.

I was scheduled to take a mid-term exam at seminary the Monday after the funeral. My professor graciously allowed me to postpone the exam for another week. Mrs. Davis drove over from Alabama every Monday to stay with Michael so I could continue my classes and complete the fall term. He was old enough to stay by himself but was having a hard time dealing with his father's death. I decided to skip the winter term of school in order to be home for Michael. I also had to deal with all the paperwork and other issues that came with losing a spouse.

As the holidays approached, I was still going through the motions. My heart was heavy and I dreaded all the effort of Thanksgiving and Christmas. The boys and I picked up Mrs. Davis in Alabama, and we all headed to Florida to stay in a beach condo so we could spend Christmas near my sisters and their families. My mother was at Jan's house, and I valiantly tried to enjoy all the festivities. But it was very easy for ne to get emotional and weepy. Jan got upset every time I cried and that made me more anxious. I was glad to get back to Georgia where I could grieve at will, while I waited for a new and better year to arrive.

CHAPTER 42

~

A Year of Grief

That new and better year did not live up to my expectations. My experience with grief was like a summer sky—one minute clear and sunny and the next cloudy and stormy. My really bad days hit when I was the least prepared, but I had no choice except to give in and let myself feel the pain. It was easy to blame myself for not doing more to intervene before Talmadge's heart attack. There had been subtle signs—shortness of breath, fatigue, and anxiety in spite of his good June doctor's report. I would've, could've, and should've plagued me at night after Michael was in bed. The lost opportunities for us as a couple due to his work hours weighed me down. And the thought of being alone with my illness was overwhelming.

One good thing about his years of work at Colonial Pipeline was generous benefits and health insurance that gave me some financial security. I asked God to forgive me for being so ungrateful for the many years he worked those difficult shifts.

It helped when I went back to school in January and became immersed in my studies. One class required me to do a ministry project for my church. I organized and implemented an adult church training program which was well received. My pastor was impressed, and as a result the church gave me a part-time job working with children's activities. I planned quarterly activities for the school-age kids and a summer camp program. My biggest challenge was coordinating a huge fall festival sponsored by the church for the surrounding community. I plowed through in spite of my fatigue and grief. I knew in order for me to get a full time job after seminary, I had to have practical experience.

After my Father's death, Mother became entirely dependent on the help of her Burke neighbors. She didn't drive and needed help getting to the grocery store and her doctors' offices. Somehow, each fall she managed to stay well long enough to fly south to escape the long, isolating winters of upstate New York. My sisters and I finally convinced her that she needed to move south permanently. Jan rented a small apartment for her in Gulf Breeze, Florida where she and Audrey had homes. We three girls headed north to sort and clean out Mother's house and arrange for the move. It was not easy for her since she would be leaving friends and family behind. She would also have to acclimate to the hot and humid Florida summers. Jan, Audrey, and I loved it since we could go visit, take her out to lunch or shopping, and know that she had family close by to meet her needs.

After seven months of living in Florida, Mother decided to go back up north to visit for the summer. She was at her sister Gert's house in Malone, New York when she collapsed and died on August 28, 1987 at the age of seventy-seven. The autopsy showed that she had suffered an enlarged heart probably due to the large doses of asthma sprays she had used over the years. Like my father, she got her wish to die close to Burke.

We held a memorial service for her in the Methodist Church under the watchful protection of those beautiful stained-glass windows. We sang "How Great Thou Art," then we buried her next to my father. At the funeral I read a poem I had written six years earlier.

A Mother's Day Tribute

I thought and thought what I could do
to celebrate your day.
You said you didn't want a gift
for which I'd have to pay.
So I decided a poem to write
would be the thing to do.
I'd recall my growing up years
and share my love for you.

You carefully mended all my socks,
You nursed me through the chicken pox.
At dinner time I ate good food,
A meatloaf or chicken that you had stewed.

The dress for the prom and the high school ring,
I never lacked for a single thing.
You made the chocolate cakes and treats,
For every occasion that called for eats.

You hemmed my skirts and fixed the rips,
To cover up my too-big hips.
You quizzed me for each history test,
And encouraged me to do my best.

When someone was sick or had a need,
You sent a card or did a good deed.
This taught me very early in life,
To care of others involved in strife.

Where boys were concerned, I admit you were strict,
And sometimes it would cause conflict.
But I don't regret now having some rules,
They kept me from going the way of some fools.

In more recent years when my sons were born,
And I from a lack of sleep was worn,
You'd give the bottles and calm their cries,
And I would relax and close my eyes.

A card for all the special days
Or a gift would show in many ways,
That you'd recalled a special event,
And through the mail a remembrance sent.

Keeping house when I had my surgery,
And cooking and washing during an emergency.
Writing recipes and helping prepare,
The boys' special diet with extra care.

All of the above are just a few
Of the many things you have tried to do,
To make my days a little carefree,
And give me time just to be me.

So here's my wish for you today in 1981.
I hope this May 10th Mother's Day is a very special one.
Although I'm not as creative
As Helen Steiner Rice,
I tried my best to write this poem
And make it just as nice.

—Frieda Davis

CHAPTER 43

Scattered Pieces

After leaving Mother's funeral and being surrounded by family and friends, I dreaded returning home. The boys had not flown with me to the funeral, but had stayed with friends in Marietta. As I got off the plane in Atlanta and made my way to baggage claim, I felt bereft and alone. In four years, I had buried my father, my husband, and now my mother, and as far as I knew, I would be the next one buried. Someone from my church picked me up and drove me home. Now it was going to be up to me to pick up the scattered puzzle pieces of my life and trust God to see my sons and me through the difficult days ahead.

So many changes in such a short time span were hard to absorb. Then Stuart announced that he wanted to leave the engineering program at Georgia Tech to pursue a finance and business degree at the University of Georgia. It meant he would no longer be home every other quarter and that he would be moving to Athens, Georgia. I had depended on him a great deal since his dad's death, and now it was time for him and me to move on.

Michael continued to struggle in high school, especially with math. I hired a tutor to get him up to speed so he could pass those tough exams.

Now, I had the full responsibility for house and car maintenance, plus working part time, and finishing seminary. My liver disease symptoms were bearable, and somehow I managed to keep all my plates spinning at the same time.

God was teaching me to trust Him for each day's needs and to do even more— to rejoice in the midst of mounting difficulties. In February 1988, I wrote a poem about my journey.

REJOICE IN DAILY TRIALS

All around me everywhere
I see this world's despair,
Over what the future will be like,
And how I should prepare.

I feel secure in the thought;
It keeps me every day.
My hope is fixed on Jesus,
He's coming back some day!

But what about the daily trials?
They come so regularly,
Particularly death and sickness,
Do the scriptures have a key?

In Paul's book to the Romans,
Tribulations I am asked to bear.
My life can reflect God's glory,
I'll have patience more to share.

So many need encouragement,
And I've been down that road,
I can tell them about Jesus' love,
His desire to share the load.

So I'll rejoice in daily trials,
Even though it's very hard;
More hope for future glory,
Will be my sure reward.

—Frieda Davis

Jan, Frieda, Audrey, Jack – 1989

CHAPTER 44

A New Ministry

An Associate's Degree in Religious Education was bestowed on me in May, 1988. I met Jan and Audrey in Florida, and we headed to my graduation in New Orleans, Louisiana. It was a proud moment for me to accomplish my goal under such difficult circumstances. For my graduation gift, my friend Shirley took me on an all-expenses paid trip to the Bahamas. In typical fashion, I ended up with an intestinal illness after pouring a canned Coke over local ice.

After returning to Georgia, I received a call from my pastor telling me about a full-time Minister of Education position at a Baptist church in Stone Mountain, Georgia. They wanted a woman to fill that role. With my freshly signed seminary degree still rolled up in the tube, I met with the Minister of Education search committee. I was full of enthusiasm and confidence as I explained my philosophy of religious education and my ideas for creating a great education program for the church. The committee let me know they were looking for someone with maturity and experience. I told them I was a middle-age woman with grown children, and that I had years of experience in volunteer church work.

During the vetting process, I also told them that I had health issues and the long drive from my house to the church would be challenging for me, but I knew I could do it. Since I had mastered the ability to push through in spite of my fatigue, most people couldn't tell by looking at me how bad I felt. My determined spirit must have impressed them. After two interviews with the search committee, I was offered a call to serve as Minister of Education. The committee said, "You are just what we're looking for."

White Oak Hills Baptist Church in Stone Mountain, Georgia was forty-five miles from my house in Marietta—over an hour away in good traffic—and traffic was seldom good. I never was a very confident driver on Atlanta's busy interstates where most people drove well above the speed limit and switched lanes with abandon. But feeling God's leading, I accepted the position. After four difficult years dealing with grief while at the same time completing seminary, God had opened a door and given me a ministry. I felt blessed to have the opportunity to make a fresh start and fulfill what I believed was God's will for my life. Michael was entering his senior year in high school. I didn't want to move and make him change schools. It was up to me to trust him and me into God's hands, while I began the long, daily commute to my new job.

The city of Stone Mountain was named for the massively large granite outcropping that reaches over sixteen hundred feet in the air. Carved on the side of the mountain is a monument to three Confederate generals, Stonewall Jackson, Robert E. Lee, and Jefferson Davis, all astride their favorite horses. This DeKalb County community at one time had been a hot bed of Klu Klux Klan activity, but by 1988 had become a city in racial transition. People from around the world were moving into the area–Kenyans, Jamaicans, Nigerians, and Asians. White Oak Hills and its pastor, Dr. Ron Hanie, were determined to minister to the changing community. I was called to that church to help with that task.

Frieda and Audrey at Seminary Graduation

CHAPTER 45

Training and Teaching

At White Oak Hills my first assignments were to organize an effective Sunday School program for all ages and put in place a program for training church members in Baptist beliefs. Many of the church attendees were from other countries as well as other Christian denominations. They were more worship oriented and had little understanding of the purpose of Sunday School and other church educational programs. So I had a lot of teaching and training to do to bring folks into a better understanding of Baptist church life. My Sundays were long, since I had to be at the church by nine in the morning, and with evening services and meetings, I didn't get home until nine at night. Some of the single ladies or couples in the church provided lunch and a spare bedroom for a Sunday afternoon nap for me, since it was too far for me to drive back home. Some Sundays, Michael drove his car over so he could be there for church.

I planned adult activities, Vacation Bible School, and kids' summer camps. The only group I didn't work with was youth. With the help of many volunteers, I did my best to provide quality educational opportunities in the church and for the community. During Bible

School, I packed my bag and spent the week with a friend so I could be at the church early every day.

In addition, the Stone Mountain Baptist Association offered me opportunities to lead Sunday school leadership workshops. It took a lot of effort to put a conference together, but the teacher in me thrived in that type of environment. I enjoyed the work and the new people, but I knew I was pushing my body to the limit. God provided strength each day and an extra dose on those days and in those places where I needed it the most. That was usually when I was getting on the interstate every morning and evening during rush hour traffic. God opened up a lot of lanes to allow me and my big car to squeeze in and not get hit.

After Michael's high school graduation in 1989, I moved into a nice apartment in Stone Mountain. The church members were wonderful, helping me make the move and giving me a housewarming shower to equip my new apartment. Michael was now eighteen—old enough to stay by himself in the house in Marietta and commute to college. I drove home every Friday to spend time with him, wash our clothes, buy groceries, and pay bills. On Sunday mornings, I'd drive back to the church and my apartment to start another week. It helped being closer to my work, but taking care of two places was not easy.

My first piece of cranberry glass was purchased while I lived in Stone Mountain. One piece doesn't make a collection, and I knew I had to have more. My friends, Shirley and Libby and I planned the first of many get-a-ways to the north Georgia mountains and shopped in all the small towns along the way. We all had lists of things we were looking for, and I always came home with at least one more piece of cranberry glass. We shopped until we dropped and laughed and cried over everything happening in our lives. Those trips were like a spiritual retreat and a trip to the psychiatrist all rolled into one.

By the end of 1990, I realized my health was deteriorating. The itching increased, my weight was dropping, and I was struggling to concentrate on the tasks at hand. It had been ten years since my initial PBC diagnosis, and I tried not to think that those signs were symptomatic of advancing liver disease. But my doctor's visits confirmed my suspicions that my liver enzymes were elevated even more. Liver transplants were first performed in 1986 and by 1990 were showing good promise with the introduction of better immunosuppressing drugs. But the risk of dying from rejection or infection after the transplant was still very high. During those early years, the lifespan of most liver transplant patients was one to two years. I felt totally overwhelmed by the idea of a transplant, and I didn't like to think about someone else dying before I could live. In the meantime, I had things I wanted to accomplish before making that difficult decision.

Frieda, Judy, Libby, Shirley-Highlands, NC.

CHAPTER 46

An Uncertain Future

I t was very important to me to have my sons settled in lives of their own where they were no longer dependent on me. I was glad when Stuart married his college sweetheart, Ruth Hardie, in December 1990. Ruth's parents were missionaries in Taiwan, and so Ruth and I handled a lot of the wedding preparation details stateside. Shirley helped me choose a lovely teal dress the summer before on a trip to Savannah. In spite of the usual pre-wedding jitters and mix-ups, the wedding took place in a beautiful church surrounded by poinsettias and Christmas greens. My doctor gave me a prescription for sleep because of all the stress I was under, and it had the opposite effect and kept me awake at night. In spite of my exhaustion and regret that Stuart's dad was not with us to celebrate, my family sent the happy couple off to begin their lives together. Their first year of marriage was a real challenge, since Ruth had one more year of studies at UGA. Stuart went to work in Charlotte, N.C. for the Office of the Comptroller while Ruth lived with her grandmother near Athens, GA.

During 1991, I realized my living arrangements had to change. I was spending more than I was earning by maintaining two separate residences. I put my house in Marietta on the market and started house shopping in the Stone Mountain area. It was my heart's desire, but not God's best for me. He was looking out for me in ways I could not see at the time. I couldn't find an affordable house in Stone Mountain and nobody was looking at my house in Marietta.

In early fall, I became very sick with a serious intestinal bug. The pain was unbearable, and Ruth rushed me to the emergency room. A week in the hospital taking powerful antibiotics convinced me that my health was in jeopardy. The lab reports on the status of my liver were not good, and my doctor suggested a return trip to the Mayo Clinic for a follow-up evaluation. Libby and I flew to Rochester, Minnesota in October, 1991. That was the year the Atlanta Braves defeated the Minnesota Twins in the World Series. Libby and I were the only people in Minnesota cheering for the Braves.

Once again, I made the rounds of the doctors in the Mayo Clinic and underwent a new series of tests. One extensive test was used to determine the amount of my remaining liver function. Libby was a great help and encouragement during that difficult testing process. Based on the test results, the Mayo doctors told me I had approximately two more years before I would need a transplant. I gained a lot of information about the effectiveness of transplants for PBC patients, but was also warned that it would be difficult to get one. I literally would have to be "falling off the cliff" and hope that the right liver would be available at the right time and place to save my life.

Since Emory University Hospital in Georgia was closest to me, I was advised to get an appointment with their transplant team as soon as possible. The advice of the Mayo Clinic doctors helped me realize it was time to get serious about getting a liver transplant. I had no choice but to put myself at the complete mercy of God and His plan for my life. I knew if He wanted me to live, I would get a donor liver. If that was not His plan, I would die and go to a better place to be with Him. But either way, I was not looking forward to the process.

Another decision was clarified in my mind. I had to get off the treadmill of work and stress. I turned in my resignation at White Oak

Hills effective December 15, 1991. It was a difficult decision, but one that I had to make. The church was struggling with the loss of many members due to racial transition in the community. It was the right decision for me and for the church finances. With my precarious health, my priorities had to change. Taking better care of my health and helping Michael get through college and on his own was now my prime focus. The people at White Oak Hills gave me a great send off by giving me a small Christmas tree with $20 bills clipped all over it. They packed up my apartment and moved my furniture back to my house in Marietta. I applied for Social Security disability insurance and went home to a very uncertain future.

Part Three

"For I know the plans I have for you, declares the Lord, plans to prosper you and not to harm you, plans to give you hope and a future" (Jeremiah 29:11).

CHAPTER 47

A Time to Forgive

After my initial diagnosis of liver disease in 1982, I had asked myself, *What does God want me to do with the rest of my life?* That answer had sent me to seminary and to an opportunity to work in religious education. It had been struggle to get through school, grieve the deaths of my parents and husband, and establish myself in a church staff position, but I believe it was the challenge and the desire to do what God called me to do that kept me going. For ten years keeping busy with school and work had helped me stay in denial about my future. But by the end of 1991, my body and brain were struggling to survive. In addition, I wasn't making enough money to maintain two residences and my high-mileage car stayed constantly in need of repair.

Within a month after my retirement and returning to my house in Marietta, I received calls from two different churches wanting me to send resumes and talk with their search committees. One was a former church wanting to hire me as a full time children's minister and another out-of-state church was looking for a female Minister of Education. Telling them I was not available because of my health was extremely painful.

Once the busyness crutch was removed, a dark shadow of grief began to settle around me again like a shroud. Grief work is never easy but is very necessary. Anger is a big part of grief and I had plenty of it. I was angry at my dead parents for never listening to me about how their extended annual visits put a strain on our marriage. I was angry at Talmadge for never listening to me about his destructive rotating shifts and his smoking. I was angry that much of my close family support was gone, and I felt abandoned and left to cope with my terminal illness alone. I felt terribly disappointed that my career had been cut short and that my seminary education was going to waste.

During the first three months of my forced retirement, I slept. I tried to pray and read my Bible for encouragement, but deep down I was disappointed and angry that God had allowed these difficulties to overwhelm my life. Slopping around in pajamas and a robe didn't help my mood, so every day I showered, got dressed, and put on makeup. Shopping had always been therapy for me and my fallback attempt at self-help. However, money was tight and my energy in short supply, so I tried to stay out of stores. It was all I could do to buy groceries. About the time I got to the store, a body draining fatigue would set in.

On one occasion, I broke down crying in the middle of the grocery store and knew I couldn't drive home. In those days before cell phones I was stuck, but then one of God's small miracles appeared. My friend, Libby, came around the corner pushing her buggy, took one look at me, and drove me home. Later she took Michael back to get my car and bring home my groceries.

It was time to get professional help to deal with my grief so I could move on with whatever time I had left. A Christian counselor helped me deal with my anger issues. My biggest challenge was to forgive those family members that I felt had abandoned me and were no longer alive to defend themselves.

The Hiding Place by Corrie Ten Boom came to my mind. She and her sister, Betsy, had spent years in a German concentration camp during WWII as a punishment for hiding Jews from the Nazis. Betsy had been in the death chambers, and Corrie had struggled to forgive the brutal guard who had been so cruel to her. She realized that forgiveness is a gift from God, and since she had received forgiveness through Jesus, she could extend that gift to the guard as well. Rereading that book helped me put my anger in perspective. Jesus forgave all my many sins–past, present, and future. Now it was up to me, with Jesus' help, to extend that same grace to my deceased family members. A great burden was lifted, and I was able to move forward once again.

Listening to Christian music also helped me regain my spiritual perspective. The music lulled me to sleep at night and put a spring in my step during the day. I loaded cassettes of praise music, hymns, and worship songs into my boom box and carried it with me from one room to the other. Whether I was cleaning, resting, or soaking in the bathtub, the empty house was filled with music. I cried and sang at the top of my lungs. When there was a beat to the song and my energy allowed, I danced around the room. "God Will Make a Way," "Majesty," and "In His Time," were my favorite choruses. The words of the old hymn, "God Will Take Care of You," by Civilla Martin also spoke to my heart.

"Be not dismayed whate'er betide, God will take care of you; beneath his wings of love abide, God will take care of you."

CHAPTER 48

Preparing for an Empty Nest

Michael completed his junior year at the Atlanta College of Art while still living at home. He was dating a girl he met from Ragland, Alabama where Talmadge had been born. Every weekend he either drove to Alabama to see Wendy or she drove over to spend the weekend with us. Michael and I had lived separately for two years, so it was an adjustment for us to be back in each other's space. I had always been overly protective of him because of his allergies and struggles with depression, but it was time to back off and let him mature. He needed to learn independence so he could survive with or without me. I knew I had to find something else to do with my life other than worry about my son.

I started looking for a new church. For six years I'd served on a church staff, and prior to that had volunteered numerous times for key church positions. Now I needed to find a place to worship where I could just be me. My preference was to find a small church, since that was my lifelong habit, but none felt like home. For several Sundays I visited Smyrna First Baptist Church, one of the largest churches in my area. I occupied an obscure pew in the balcony so no one would recognize me or care that I was there. My need was for a church to minister to me instead of requiring anything from me. That church's singles' ministry was also very appealing.

It was surprising to find so many other singles in my age group involved in the church. Some were wounded souls who had hoped to marry but had been denied that opportunity. Others bore scars from one or more painful divorces, and a few were widows like I was. Some were looking to the church for dating or marriage opportunities. Others wanted to participate in Bible studies and fun-filled activities with like-minded singles. Thirty years had passed since my last experience in the single life. I wasn't sure how much in common I would have with the other singles and if they would accept me since I was battling a terminal illness.

I decided a new venture in my life was just what I needed, so I joined the church and became an active participant in a singles' coed Sunday school class. It took me a while to open up, but as I did, I received compassion and support from the members. I owe those people a debt of gratitude for teaching me how to laugh again. We had a lot of fun playing cards and participating in church-sponsored group activities.

Michael graduated from college in May 1993 and found a job soon after. I could breathe knowing he could support himself when I was no longer around. He also proposed to Wendy, and they planned their wedding for April 1994. My nest was soon to be empty, and I breathed a sigh of relief that my full-time parenting days were about over. I needed to focus on my health and well-being. I thanked God that he had allowed me to live long enough to see my sons educated, working, and settled. I felt that my work on earth was done and was at peace if God decided to take me home to heaven. But if God still had something for me to do, I was more than willing to stick around a while longer.

CHAPTER 49

So Long Spleen

I was still wavering about wanting a transplant and put off making an appointment with the Emory Transplant Center. Part of my problem was related to Emory's location. It took forty-five minutes on Atlanta freeways to get there in good traffic and much longer in one of Atlanta's notorious traffic pileups. My driving skills were not good, my reaction time was slow, and many times I had brain fog and couldn't remember where I was or how I got there. Although they would have been willing, I didn't want to burden my friends to drive me to the transplant center. However, I could no longer ignore my increasing symptoms. Brain confusion, fatigue, and increased itching were signs that my disease was advancing. I realized I needed to make that appointment at Emory soon if I expected to live.

My body decided not to wait for my brain to decide about a transplant. One day I blew my nose and blood gushed out and would not stop. I drove myself to the Kennestone Hospital emergency room where I was admitted with an almost non-existent blood platelet level. After a lecture from my doctor about the dangers of driving with a low platelet level, I spent a week in the hospital on blood transfusions. The goal was to rebuild my platelet level and determine the cause of my problem. Tests revealed that my spleen was no longer working, so the doctors put me on steroids in an attempt to restore function. That drug and I didn't get along; I couldn't sleep and felt paranoid all the time. The steroids depleted my immune system, and soon I ended up back in the hospital with pneumonia.

At the end of 1993, the doctors agreed that it was time to remove my spleen. I was told that not having a spleen was a risk factor for receiving a successful liver transplant since the spleen was vital in fighting infection. It was a risk I had to take. The side effects of the steroids were unbearable, and I didn't want to live like that.

My surgery was scheduled for December 15 so that I could be home before Christmas. In my typical fashion, I decorated the house for the holidays, bought and wrapped everyone's Christmas gifts, sent out cards, and baked Christmas goodies. I was totally exhausted by the time I was admitted to the hospital for surgery.

I left the hospital on schedule, three days before Christmas. Libby stayed to take care of me and, after one night at home, we realized I was in serious trouble. My stomach had doubled in size and my long abdominal incision was opening. Libby took me back to the hospital, where I was readmitted. So much fluid had built up in my abdomen, I looked nine months pregnant. The fluid or ascites was another sign of advancing liver disease. The doctors prescribed a heavy dose of diuretics and wrapped my belly in bandages that soaked through in ten minutes. All the fluid was leaking out of my incision. After spending Christmas in the hospital, I was sent home to deal with my condition. There was no way I could take care of myself. All I could do was lie in the bed and leak through my incision. Libby stayed with me for several days, changing my bandages every half hour. Shirley came for another week to wait on me hand and foot. I was helpless and totally dependent on the mercy of my friends.

If I had thought getting rid of my spleen would fix my problems, I had been badly mistaken. By the middle of January 1994, the fluid was gone, but I was struggling to get back on my feet. The fluid build-up had rearranged my other internal organs which resulted in bladder and female issues. In the meantime, I had Michael's wedding to prepare for. Libby drove me to Ragland in February to meet Wendy's family and to make arrangements with a caterer for the rehearsal dinner. Libby and her daughter offered to decorate for the dinner. With no energy to shop, I decided to wear the same mother-of-the-groom dress I had worn to Stuart's wedding.

I didn't want to do anything to interfere with the wedding plans, since I was very anxious for Michael to get married and be on his own. I wanted to face my own tenuous future not worrying about him. In addition, Stuart and Ruth told me I was going to be a grandmother, and I prayed that God would grant me enough time to see that baby.

My desire for order and having all the loose ends tied up was very strong. I believed I could go meet the Lord if my earthly affairs were in order. But that was just wishful thinking. One week before Michael's wedding, I started running a high fever and had labored breathing. I ended up back in the hospital with double pneumonia and was started on strong antibiotics. My greatest fear, that my illness would interfere with the wedding, had become reality. The doctors advised me against leaving the hospital too early, but I insisted I be at the wedding and told them I would have plenty of help. Audrey and George came to help me get ready for the wedding. They drove me to Alabama, where I supervised while Libby and her daughter decorated for the rehearsal dinner. I pushed through my exhaustion and the wedding went off as scheduled.

After the wedding, it took several weeks to recover from the hospitalizations and medications. I had become an official empty nester and told the Lord that I felt my work on earth was done. I had defied the odds by surviving for twelve years with PBC. But just in case I had some more time left, I decided to arrange a consultation with the liver transplant team at Emory. Libby drove me to my appointment and stayed with me while I learned what my next steps would be to qualify for a transplant. After numerous tests by the Emory team, I was told that I wasn't yet a candidate for a new liver, but to stay in touch with the transplant team on a regular basis.

Marcella Davis was born in October 1994, making me a first-time grandmother. It was exciting when Stuart and Ruth brought her to visit me for the first time.

CHAPTER 50

Time on My Hands

Waiting with nothing to do was not one of my strong points. My singles' Sunday school class was in need of a teacher. Since I had too much time on my hands, I took on the challenge of teaching the weekly Bible lessons. As the teacher, I received the greatest blessing due to the amount of prayer and preparation I put into each lesson. That role also provided me the opportunity to minister to others. I could weep and cry with others going through illness or despair. I could rejoice and laugh with those who had an answer to prayer. I knew God wanted me to be a positive influence for Him, and that class provided me with a new ministry.

Opportunities for dating within the single's department opened up, and I enjoyed going out to eat and to the movies—something I hadn't done in a long time. However, most of the men I met had a lot of excess baggage from previous relationships, and I didn't need or want that in my life. I always tried to conduct myself in a way pleasing to the Lord, because I knew how vulnerable I was and how easily tempted I could be.

I became fast friends with Marianne, a singles' class member. She had been through a painful divorce and was beginning to sprout her single wings, and she needed a partner in crime. She kept encouraging me to go places with her and get more involved in the social scene. More than once I dragged myself out of the house to go someplace she wanted to go, thinking it would be good for both of us. Marianne especially enjoyed dancing, but finding a wholesome dancing place for two older single women was not easy. I hadn't danced in years but had always loved it when I was a teenager. The local Methodist church had Bible studies and classes for singles every Monday night, followed by dancing. Most weeks Marianne picked me up in her red sports car and we headed for the church. I did learn to do some of the country line dances, so I at least got into motion. Most of the time, all I needed was paste to make me the official wall flower. Occasionally, a man would ask me to dance, but I spent most of my time watching Marianne whirl around the dance floor with one suitor after another.

CHAPTER 51

God's Phone Call

June 3, 1995 was a warm, sunny day in Marietta. Facing another day alone and not feeling good was a way of life for me. Staying in bed was not an option; I needed a plan for my day—something to keep me motivated and moving.

In spite of my overwhelming desire that day to be a couch potato, I put on my bathing suit and headed for the YWCA to swim a few laps. The rhythmic motion of my arms and legs as I propelled myself from one end of the pool to the other gave me plenty of time to think about the challenges I'd faced in recent years. Five hospitalizations in the past year plus major surgery to remove my spleen had left me depleted physically and financially, and the battle was far from over. I felt like a wounded soldier with a post-traumatic stress disorder. The doctors said if I survived long enough and someone else died that matched, I would be redeployed to the war zone—back to the hospital to receive a liver transplant. I tried to focus on my blessings and not think about my losses and what I would yet face, but as I swam grief came back to haunt me like a recurring bad dream.

Fatigue forced me from the pool after only a few laps. Like a wet dog that's had a good swim, I tried to shake off the water and my feeling of impending doom. After a warm shower, I headed for the grocery store and the bank. By the time I made it home, I was exhausted. After lunch I laid down for a nap but woke up barely able to get off the couch. Something was wrong, and my foggy brain was confused. *What day was it?* I finally remembered it was Friday. With the weekend coming, I knew I should call my doctor. Otherwise, I would end up in the hospital emergency room. Weekend visits to the local emergency room were the ultimate torture. The last time I had been there, police had been swarming the place as shooting victims were being admitted. I hyperventilated just thinking about it.

I described my aching body and feverish symptoms to my doctor's nurse. She said, "You probably have the flu. Drink plenty of liquids, take some Advil, and come to the office on Monday if you're not any better." That was not good medical advice for a person with a terminal liver disease. I thought about calling the doctor back and insisting on seeing him immediately, but I didn't feel like arguing with the nurse. I did have the presence of mind to call my youngest son, Michael, using speed dial on the phone. I reached him at work and told him I was sick, but since he was used to having a sick mother, no alarm bells sounded.

The portable phone was in my hand as I staggered upstairs and fell across the bed. My bedroom was dark when I awoke from a drugged sleep. I reached for the bedside lamp but was so dizzy I couldn't lift my head off the pillow to turn it on. As I clutched the phone receiver, I tried in vain to think of someone's phone number. My voice was gone, and my mind was completely blank. I silently lifted a prayer as I felt death creeping through my body.

Lord, if you want me to live, get me help!

In desperation and with my last ounce of strength, I slapped the phone keypad. Miraculously, I heard the phone ring on the other end. Mrs. Davis, my mother-in-law in Alabama, said "Hello."

I squeaked, "I'm sick and need help."

"Frieda?" she asked recognizing my squeak.

"Help!"

"I'll call Michael," she said.

Michael and Wendy's apartment was about ten minutes away. My front door was locked and Michael was the only person with a key. Soon he was at my bedside calling an ambulance. The next few hours were a blur as I was admitted to the emergency room, where tests were run, and vital signs were recorded. I later learned that my blood pressure had been 60/30 when the paramedics got to me. My doctor soberly said, "Mrs. Davis, we are putting you in ICU." Even in my weakened condition, I tried to talk him out of it.

"If you want to live, you are going to ICU. Mrs. Davis, you are a very sick woman."

I floated in and out of consciousness for days, while bags of intravenous fluids were dripping into my body. The twenty-four hour bright lights and the constant noise of a droning television were unwelcome intrusions. The inside and outside of my mouth were so painful and dry I could barely make a sound. Later, I learned that I had so many fever blisters on my mouth and face I was unrecognizable. Numerous white coated doctors and nurses wearing scrubs poked and prodded every inch of my body. I hoarsely whispered to every doctor and nurse who came to my bedside, "What's wrong with me?" My anxiety level rose every time no answer was given.

On my third day in ICU, the visiting doctor was interrupted by a technician who ran into my room, "We have a culture. It's Strep Sepsis," she said.

"Change the antibiotics," the doctor ordered the nurse outside the door.

Then he turned and soberly spoke to me, "Is there anyone the hospital needs to call? We suspect an intestinal blockage and with a very serious infection, you are too weak for surgery."

In my gravelly voice, I told the doctor, "God saved my life. I'm not going to die."

There was no doubt in my mind God had dialed the phone number that saved me from certain death.

"Someone was looking out for you," he said. "You had less than two hours to live when you were admitted. All your vital organs were shutting down."

Overwhelming peace wrapped around me like a warm, cozy blanket. It was beyond my comprehension to grasp how the great and wonderful God of heaven intervened to save my life. I began to relax and pray, thanking God that my digestive system was waking up, and that I would be spared surgery. Over and over I prayed as much of the Twenty-Third Psalm as I could remember, but I couldn't put the verses in order no matter how hard I tried. However, I knew I had walked "through the valley of the shadow of death," (v.4a) and had confidence that God's "goodness and mercy would follow me" (v.6a) all the remaining days of my life.

CHAPTER 52

Back on My Feet

Michael and his wife periodically showed up at my bedside in ICU. It was obvious they were frightened by all the pumps, bags of IV fluids, and my emaciated state. I tried to assure them I was going to be alright. I wanted to talk to Stuart, but he had moved to Charlotte, North Carolina and there was no phone in the room. As my oldest and take charge son, I needed him to communicate with the doctors on my behalf. After pestering the ICU personnel, they brought a phone to my room so I could call him. Michael had not really explained to him the gravity of my situation. Stuart made plans to drive to Marietta as soon as his demanding job would allow.

The intensive care unit of the hospital was a very lonesome place, even with all the bustle of medical personnel. Visitors were admitted only two or three times each day. I found myself alone most of the time, watching more and more television and listening to the clock tick from one second to the next. Two news reports on CNN Headline News captured my attention.

Mickey Mantle had been the New York Yankees' most celebrated baseball player. He had been regarded by many to be one of the greatest baseball players of all time. Most of his fans, however, had not known about his sordid personal life and his lifelong battle with alcoholism. In 1994 he had been told that alcohol had destroyed his liver and that he had to give up drinking or die. In June 1995, he had been placed on the National Liver Transplant organ list and moved to the top of the list. That was a very controversial move because many felt that his fame and fortune had allowed him to bypass others on the transplant list. He received his liver transplant on June 8, 1995 while I struggled to survive in ICU. I have to admit I was upset about it because earlier that year I had joined a pre-transplant support group and was aware of many who were suffering and waiting for their turn. Mantle would only live two more months with his transplanted liver, but during those two months he turned his life around by making a profession of faith in Jesus.

Another inspirational story capturing news headlines the first week of June 1995 was about Captain Scott O'Grady, an Air Force pilot who had ejected from an F-16 fighter jet in Europe. His plane had been shot down by Serbians while he was on patrol during a NATO mission over Bosnia. The Marines had spent days trying to locate and rescue him from enemy territory. The brave rescue took place on June 8, 1995 during my stay in ICU. After his capture, O'Grady said his life was spared as an answer to prayer. "I prayed to God and asked him for a lot of things, and he delivered throughout the entire time," O'Grady told reporters.

Both news events inspired me during those long, lonely, and difficult days when I was held captive in ICU. Like Scott O'Grady, I knew God had saved my life, and like Mickey Mantle, I felt I would receive a liver transplant in God's timing. I received one other good piece of news on

June 8. The doctor heard bowel sounds and said that I would be spared surgery. My body was responding positively to the antibiotics and my life was saved.

Stuart drove from Charlotte, got me out of ICU, and finally released from the hospital. I was so weak and emaciated that the doctors would only let me go if I had full time care. Jan and Curt came up to help me for the first week and Audrey the next. Jan took one look at me and said in her unique way, "My God, you look like you've been in a concentration camp."

I ate baby food around the clock to regain my strength. Then I graduated to soft scrambled eggs and potato broth that Curt delivered to my room day and night. A trip to the bathroom required a walker and an additional person to help me balance. A week later, I was able to go down the stairs by sitting down and bumping one step at a time.

Curt called me Job, the character in the Bible that suffered so much loss and physical affliction. I responded to him that I was "Jobette," and that just as God had better things in mind for Job, there were better things in my future as well.

My sisters worried a lot about my health. After spending so much time with them, I became concerned about their health as well. Jan was ten years older, and she didn't take good care of herself. She was a heavy smoker and ate a lot of high-fat, carbohydrate-rich foods. Her weight had ballooned and she had difficulty going up and down the stairs in my house. Audrey, on the other hand, ate well and was physically fit. But the more we talked, I realized how fatigued she was and when she described her itchy skin to me, the more alarmed I became. I urged her to get tested for Primary Biliary Cirrhosis, the same disease I had. We both realized that the chances of her having the same condition were remote, but I urged her to check it out. The research on PBC showed a possible genetic link in families, and that the disease can be passed down through the family line—especially to the female members. Seeing the condition I was in, it's no wonder she was in no hurry to get tested.

CHAPTER 53

A Healing Retreat

Audrey and George invited me to continue my recuperation at their camp in the Adirondack Mountains. They picked me up on their way to New York in July, and I settled into the peace and quiet of their mountain retreat. I enjoyed Audrey's good cooking and relaxed on their screened porch listening to the breezes rustling the trees. One afternoon I walked down to the edge of the water on their property. Like sparkling diamonds, the bright rays of the sun danced over Gull Pond. Red, gold, and yellow tinged trees climbed the sloping hills and reflected on the eerily still water. A flock of Canadian geese broke their arrow formation, descended to drink and fish, and then fiercely flapped to regain altitude for the flight south. With all this beauty of God's world displayed before me, part of me was very grateful to be alive to enjoy the splendor. The rest of me feared this would be my last time to see this beautiful place.

As I reflected and prayed about my past and future in that quiet and peaceful place, I recalled that Christmas many years ago in Webster when our tree had been on life support and all the needles had fallen in a heap on the floor. Just as my earthly father had saved that Christmas by getting me a new tree, my heavenly Father miraculously had saved my life. He had allowed me to get to the hospital on time and kept me from certain death while I was on life support. My heart's desire was to be like that fresh tree that stood tall and strong over my Christmas gifts. I asked God to use my spiritual gifts to allow me to share His message during whatever time I had left on earth.

As August ended and the last hurrah of summer descended on Gull Pond, I knew the time had come for me to go home and face my uncertain future. The peace and quiet of the mountains, and my sister's good cooking had helped to strengthen my body and spirit, but I was ready to finish my recuperation back home. I had confidence that somehow God would help me put together the scattered pieces of my life.

My brother-in-law drove me to the small airport in Saranac Lake, New York. The picturesque log cabin terminal was nestled among the colorful rolling hills. I boarded an eight passenger commuter jet and waved goodbye to my family as the plane taxied down the single runway. On the non-stop jet ride out of Albany, New York back to Atlanta, I took time to read, pray, and contemplate my future. The Atlanta skyline was visible on my right as we approached Hartsfield-Jackson Airport. The trees were still green and weeks away from changing, and I missed the colorful maples of upstate New York. The late summer muggy heat hit me in the face as Michael and l left the terminal and headed for his car. As we drove away onto the interstate highway, the cool breezes from the rustling mountain trees and the peaceful views of Gull Pond become only a distant memory.

What surprised me most on my return to Georgia was how well I felt. I actually experienced more good days than bad, which wasn't normal for me. I eagerly jumped back into teaching my Sunday School class and started going places with some of the men and women in the singles' department. I had regained a healthy weight and looked better than I had in a long time. In spite of the seriousness of my liver disease, my skin and eyes resisted the yellow tint that is typical of cirrhosis. I deluded myself into believing that maybe the worst was over. When

I reported in to the doctors at Emory and told them about my near death experience with Sepsis, they agreed it was a miracle I survived the ordeal. They also convinced me that I still had more hurdles to overcome.

CHAPTER 54

Saint Superman

As 1995 came to a close, I looked forward to another year and was anxious to see what opportunities God would bring into my life. Like a jolt out of the blue, I started thinking about the possibility of another marriage. I had just come through a near-death experience with Strep Sepsis and was well aware that unless I received a successful liver transplant, my days on earth were numbered. I was a middle-aged widow out of work, out of shape, and almost out of time. How dare I even think about the possibility of another marriage? But the thought wouldn't leave me alone.

As a Christian, I believed in celibacy and managed to keep myself free from temptation and a physical relationship outside of marriage. Some of my Christian friends thought I took the Bible too seriously on that subject. A casual or live-in relationship was not for me; I wanted to get married again. However, I could think of a million reasons why it would never happen. First of all, I was too sick to take care of myself, let alone think about sharing my life with another person. Secondly, what man in his right mind marries someone who might not survive two more years?

In order to put the matter to rest, I took out a piece of paper and wrote a list of my qualifications for a future marriage partner. Not wanting to be "unequally yoked" added one more challenge to the search. By the time I finished my list, it looked like a resume for Saint Superman—a committed Christian man with such fine qualities he could have his pick of women. Why would such a person choose me? I put that list on my Bible, got on my knees, and prayed for God to search throughout all His creation and to put all the resources of the universe at my disposal. My prayer to God was big and bold, "Lord, if you want me to marry again, search throughout your world and find just the right person for me. If in the remote possibility that such a man exists, bring that man into my life." The list was stored in my bedside table and my requirements for a marriage partner left in God's hands.

My friend, Marianne, was always on the go and wanting me to go too. I returned with her to the Monday night dances as well as other singles' activities at our church. We welcomed in 1996 at a midnight dance at a local apartment clubhouse in north Marietta. The music was good, but I spent most of the time sitting at a table with few opportunities to dance. I made up my mind that I wouldn't put myself through that torture again.

On March 4, 1996, I woke up with a headache and felt bad all over. I struggled to get out of bed and spent much of the day lying on the couch with a cold cloth on my head. I prayed I was not getting another serious infection. My positive attitude and confidence in God's plan for my life were on the back burner. I felt sad as I looked out my bay window at the daffodils and red tulips struggling to break through the cold ground. I identified with their struggle to break free, and it occurred to me that I might not be around to see another spring. Tears trickled down my cheeks.

"Pull yourself together. No one gets to decide how long they will live. God's in charge and in control," I announced to the four walls of my living room, hoping to hear an "Amen." I was feeling very sorry for myself when the phone rang.

"It's Marianne, and we're going dancing tonight!"

I interrupted, "I feel too bad to go anywhere, especially to a dance. I'm having a bad day, and I'm not even sure anymore that as a Sunday School teacher I should be out dancing anyway."

She was not buying my excuse. "You've got to go, and if you get out you will feel better. Get ready and I'll pick you up at 5:00."

We grabbed a bite to eat and headed for the Methodist Church on the Marietta Square. In the parking lot, I came up with every excuse I could think of for not going in. Marianne shot down all my excuses and finally won me over.

"It's cold out here," she said. "At least come in where it's warm."

I assumed my normal position at a corner table observing the festivities. When the line dancing started, I joined in and found the exercise helped me feel better. A man asked me to dance a swing song that left me winded and catching my breath. I sat down and was tapping my toes to the music when another man approached requesting a dance. Fortunately, it was a slow song so I agreed. Maybe the wall flower glue wasn't sticking so tightly after all.

"Where do you go to church?" he asked, catching me by surprise. The first question from previous dance partners had been, "How long have you been divorced?"

"I teach singles at Smyrna First Baptist," I said as we moved around the dance floor.

"I teach, too, at Burnt Hickory Baptist. I started teaching after my wife died," my dance partner said.

The coincidence surprised me, and I explained that I, too, was widowed. The song quickly came to an end, and as we thanked each other for the dance, he asked, "Can I call you sometime to talk about our classes."

"Sure!" I watched him cross the dance floor and rejoin his table and sit next to another woman. *Fat chance I'll ever hear from him again*, I thought. The evening was beginning to wind down when I wrote my phone number on a napkin and mustered up my courage to walk across the room and hand it to him. The other woman was nowhere around, so I said I'd like him to call. He pulled out a business card and wrote his home phone number on the back.

"What just happened in there?" Marianne asked as we walked to the car.

"I met a very nice man, and he said he was going to call me," I said.

""Where is the lady that I had to drag into the dance. I'd better go back and find her," Marianne joked.

CHAPTER 55

A New Lease on Life

I jumped every time the phone rang during the next few days. With no caller ID, I had no idea who was calling and was disappointed by every call that wasn't from Charles Dixon. Even though I had his phone number, I was old-fashioned and believed a man had to make the first move. I was also a master at negative thinking and had convinced myself that my dancing partner was history. "It was for the best," I told myself. With my medical history, I had no right to impose my illness on anyone else. His phone call several days later changed all that.

"Let's meet for lunch," he suggested. After discussing where each of us lived and what would be a good halfway location, we decided on the Olive Garden on Cobb Parkway in Marietta. I was surprised to learn that he lived in Kennesaw, Georgia, about twenty miles northwest of my house.

Two times around a dance floor wasn't enough time to get a mental picture of someone you had just met, so I was nervous as I drove to the restaurant. The lunch was good, and we were so absorbed in conversation, we paid no attention to the time. Three hours later, Charles brought up a subject I was least expecting.

"Have you ever thought about getting married again?"

I blushed as I stumbled to answer. "I would really have to believe it was God's will for my life."

"Do you have any say so in the matter?" he asked.

The waiters needed to be paid, and they were eager to clean up our table. I muttered a non-committal reply as he picked up the ticket.

"Maybe we can do this again sometime," he said.

"I'd like that," I said as we walked to the parking lot.

I was a wreck by the time I got home. The marriage question had unnerved me and had let me know Charles did not want to waste his time and money on a woman who was not marriageable material. He was a man on a mission to find a wife. I wanted to see him again, but I knew I couldn't lead him on and not let him know about my declining health. He had lost his first wife after a life-long battle with diabetes, and I told myself he wouldn't want to saddle himself with another sick and dying woman. It was a dilemma that drove me to my knees.

"Lord, help me to know what to do. This man wants to marry again, and I am not sure I want that for myself, and I don't want to impose my disease on him. I don't want to lead him on thinking that I am something I'm not, but I don't want to close the door either. Can't we just go out and have fun and not get serious?"

The reaction from my friends and children was not quite what I expected when I told them about my lunch date. I didn't mention that he had brought up the "M" word. Their very cautious response to the news was not excitement that I had met an interesting man, but rather that I not set myself up to get hurt. All of us believed, given my poor health, there would be no relationship for me in the near future. My negative thoughts told me they were right. My whole life had been a struggle to overcome disappointment and survive. In my weakened condition, I didn't think I could handle one more battle. And yet the desire to explore all options wouldn't leave me alone.

When I agreed to go on the next date, I knew I had to tell Charles the truth about my health. We agreed to meet for lunch and a hike at Kennesaw Mountain Battlefield Park. The national park was dedicated to the memory of those who died for both the North and South during the Civil War. In modern times Kennesaw Mountain's wooded trails around the base and to the summit make it a desirable destination for hikers and picnickers. It seemed a long way from my environment in south Cobb County and was an area I had never explored.

While we ate lunch I told Charles I had physical limitations, and I wasn't sure I could hike very far. That didn't seem to bother him. After lunch we headed for the mountain and took an easy path around the base, which was not too strenuous a climb. His strong hand felt good wrapped around mine as we walked over the rocky path.

"There's a rock outcropping up ahead," he said. "Let's sit and rest." We talked about the beautiful spring day and the budding trees all around.

"Do you know this is the Kissing Rock?" he asked.

What a line, I thought. Instead, I replied, "Are you serious?" as I looked at his twinkling eyes.

The kiss was short and sweet. The day was turning out better than I had expected.

"Do you want to go flying sometime?" he asked.

"What? You're a pilot, too! What kind of planes do you fly?" He had already told me he was an aeronautical engineer, recently retired from Lockheed Martin.

"Small light aircraft," he responded.

"Sure!" I said, throwing caution to the wind. I knew I would have plenty of time to come up with an excuse, like motion sickness or fear of heights.

"I'll call and see if there is a Lockheed Flying Club plane available," Charles said.

"Now! I didn't know you meant now!"

He looked amused, "Why not, it's a perfect day for flying."

Like a homesick angel, the two-seated plane taxied down the runway and lifted us into the cloudless sky. *What is the worst that could happen*, I asked myself? *Soon enough he would find out the truth and this will be our last date.* In the meantime, I planned to savor the thrill of the day and have some bragging rights with my lady friends. As we flew low and slow over the Kennesaw area and up toward the north Georgia Mountains, I looked down at the white-steeple churches and row upon row of *Monopoly* board houses lined up in subdivisions. *Maybe this is how God views my life. He sees the big picture and not all the little worrisome details.*

After a successful landing, we decided the day was going so well we would eat dinner. Then a movie seemed like a good idea, followed by desert before we went our separate ways. It was after midnight when I arrived home to discover multiple phone messages from Michael. "Mom where are you? Call me when you get home." When he heard about my twelve-hour date, he cautioned, "Be careful Mom. He may be after your money."

My life had taken a sudden turn for the better, and I didn't know how to handle it. I was used to dealing with adversity, illness, and rejection. The only exciting thing that had happened to me in months was getting a good night's sleep, then waking up feeling halfway decent. In spite of my best intentions, I still had not told Charles the truth about my precarious health.

CHAPTER 56

On the Mountain Top

When Charles called to say he wanted to come pick me up for church Sunday night, I dashed around the house picking up clutter and got myself ready. It was a great feeling to have a man to sit with in church. We definitely had our faith and church denomination in common. That was a real plus for me. On the way back home, Charles told me how comfortable he felt with me and asked if I wanted to go with his singles' class to a retreat in the north Georgia Mountains. I seldom planned ahead, since I was never sure how I would feel on any given day. This was different—nothing was going to keep me from going on that retreat. That would be the weekend I would tell him about my liver disease. I retrieved my Saint Superman list and began to check off my qualifications–loved the Lord God, active in church, smart with a good education, independent and not needy, good character, good to look at, lived close by, and ambitious. I, or rather God, was on a roll, and I needed to take notice. I wanted to believe He would take care of the unresolved issues as well.

The weather was cool and crisp at the mountain cottage where the group spent the weekend. We had Bible studies, played cards and board games, ate, and enjoyed each other's company. Charles and I spent most of our time with another couple our age that were also widowed and looking for companionship. Jean and Robert kept us laughing the whole weekend.

Saturday afternoon the four of us took a short hike to the waterfalls where Charles and I sat while our friends climbed up for a better view. I took a deep breath and gave him the nitty-gritty details about my liver disease and my need for a transplant. I don't know what response I expected, but I didn't think it would be good. After what seemed like an eternity he said,

"You do have health insurance, don't you?" I had to laugh, mostly from relief, but also because it was such a positive answer and not the negative reply I was expecting.

Charles then told me he had something to tell me as well. Nervously, I waited.

"I'm sixty-five and I know you are a lot younger than I am."

I was really surprised. This man had more energy than some men I knew in their forties and a whole lot more than I had at fifty-two. Of course, with my health problems, most people had more energy than I had. His face was not lined, and his thinning hair was still black. I knew he had taken early retirement from Lockheed Martin, so I had suspected he was in his late fifties.

"Age is a matter of the mind," I told him. "At our age, if we don't mind, it doesn't matter." It was a great relief to have these big issues exposed to the light of day.

That night we stole a few minutes on the cabin porch swing, where he said he was falling in love with me. I responded in kind, and we left that weekend knowing that we had a future together. The speed at which our relationship developed surprised me and came as a shock to my friends and family. I called my sisters, and Jan responded in her outspoken way,

"You've met a dancing deacon and a pilot, too. Does he have money?"

Audrey was very concerned about my health and my being fit enough to keep up with Charles' hiking, dancing, skiing, and very active lifestyle. Libby was shocked and very protective. She warned me to be careful and to tell Charles he'd better not hurt me or he'd have to deal with her."

Stuart said, "My mother has either lost her mind or is in love to go flying and on a retreat with a man she just met."

Shirley sounded very happy for me but was very practical and realistic and warned me that we should go slow and take plenty of time to get to know each other. Everyone knew how physically and emotionally vulnerable I was, and each in their own way was looking out for me.

Once we came back from the mountain top retreat, Charles and I dated every day–talking endlessly about our lives, goals, beliefs, politics, families, and finances. During one serious discussion, I asked Charles why after so many years of caring for a wife with brittle diabetes, he wanted to have a relationship with someone critically ill with liver disease.

His thoughtful response astounded me. "All the experience I gained taking care of my first wife, Mary, shouldn't go to waste. I believe God wants me to use what I've learned to take care of you."

I had spent most of my life taking care of someone else–parents, husband, and children–and now struggled to take care of myself. To think that Charles wanted to take care of me was over and above anything I wrote on my Saint Superman list. His infectious optimism was just what I needed to help me navigate the rough waters ahead. I was reminded of the Bible verse in John 10:10, "I have come that you might have life and have it more abundantly."

Three weeks after our first date, after discovering we had both prayed for the spouse that God wanted for us, Charles proposed. I accepted, and we planned our wedding for June 8, 1996—exactly one year to the day after I had been told by the ICU doctors that I would survive my ordeal with Strep Sepsis. It was also one year to the day since Scott O'Grady had been rescued from his captors and Mickey Mantle had received a new liver. After ten years of life as a critically ill widow and single parent, I began to understand why God had spared my life. He had a better future planned for me. It would be up to me to glorify

Him in all that He led me to do. Since I had no idea how many years I had left, it became my desire to make each day count.

Charles & Frieda at Toccoa Falls

CHAPTER 57

In Sickness and in Health

Charles likes to tell people that he won two proposals in the spring of 1996. The obvious one was my agreement to marry him, and the second one was the acceptance of a proposal he had made to the United States Air Force. The Small Business Innovative Research contract was for the purpose of upgrading his computer software that analyzed post-stall characteristics of various aircraft. Charles had taken short-term consulting jobs with Lockheed Martin and Georgia Tech since his retirement, but now he was ready to incorporate and move forward into his own business.

Even with his busy schedule and my health issues, we decided we wanted a real wedding celebration with family and friends. I ordered invitations, bought a dress, and planned for the reception. Shirley and Libby agreed to be my bridesmaids, and Charles asked Robert to be his best man. I enlisted my nieces to serve cake and punch.

Since we both had children, it was important to us that they be involved in the wedding. Charles' daughter was pregnant at the time and concerned about her dad marrying less than two years after her mother's death. Charles' son, Darrell and his wife, Delcina, were genuinely happy for us. Stuart and Michael liked Charles right away and were convinced that we had made the right decision. I think they were grateful that someone else would be looking after their mother. Charles' grandson, Jesse, agreed to serve as a groomsman. My daughter-in-law, Ruth Davis, was asked to sing at the wedding and Michael's wife, Wendy, was enlisted to be my wedding coordinator.

Stuart and Michael escorted me down the aisle at Burnt Hickory Baptist Church. I wore a tea length aqua lace dress, and Charles wore a tuxedo with a white vest and tie. My pastor from Smyrna First Baptist Church, Dr. Steven Kimmel, and Rev. Mike Stevens from Charles' church officiated. "For better, for worse, for richer, for poorer, in sickness and in health." With those words, we both vowed "to love and to cherish" for the rest of our lives. Those words were especially meaningful since we knew what we were facing. We realized God might grant us only a few months or years together, but we were willing to take the risk and make the most of each day. At the end of the service, there were very few dry eyes when we played the John Lennon song, "*Grow Old Along With Me, the Best is Yet to Be …God Bless Our Love.*"

We worked hard to make the wedding ceremony a time of worship as well as celebration. About two hundred people attended. Five ministers were in attendance, including my former pastors and their wives from churches where I had worked. The White Oak Hills members, where I had served as Minister of Education, loaded up their church bus and drove from Stone Mountain for the ceremony. The singles' group from Smyrna First also came in a group.

We felt blessed to have so many of our family members and our friends there to see us off as we left for our honeymoon. We drove to a resort at Stone Mountain for the weekend. While there, we found a piece of cranberry glass at an antique shop to add to my growing collection. Two days later, we flew to New York City to catch a ship headed for Bermuda. I broke Charles in really well by getting seasick on the open water in the Atlantic. He was a tried and true sailor and did everything he could to help me, but nothing worked until my feet were back on firm ground.

My house in Marietta sold quickly after the wedding, and we decided to take the proceeds from the sale and upgrade Charles' house in Kennesaw, making it into our home. We gave away a lot of things to our children and held a huge yard sale to get rid of the rest.

Our house sat on a beautiful two-acre wooded lot in west Cobb County that was like a suburban oasis. We could be in the house and yard for days on end and not see another soul. The trees were beautiful all seasons of the year. I redecorated the interior with paint, draperies, and new furnishings; upgraded the kitchen, and eventually finished a portion of the basement. Our renovated house reflected both our personalities. I can't believe we accomplished so much in the first year of our marriage. My energy level was low more days than not. I struggled with female issues related to the fluid buildup in 1993 and I stayed itchy from my liver disease. But I was happier than I had been in many years and determined to make the most of every day that Charles and I had together.

We took several business related trips pertaining to his Air Force contract and found a small space away from the house for Charles to set up his office. For my birthday in 1997, we flew to Austria to see all the places related to the *Sound of Music*. Charles also wanted to ski the Alps. It was a wonderful trip with the highlights being a horse drawn sleigh ride through the snow in the Alps and seeing the church where Maria and Captain Von Trapp were married in the movie.

We also made the decision to find a new church. We needed to make new friends together as a couple and find a place we could serve in ministry together. Both of us were interested in missions and new start churches, so we decided to join Towne View Baptist Church which was meeting in a school. In June 1997 we signed up to go with several other members on a mission trip with Builders for Christ to construct a church in Reno, Nevada. It was a dawn to dark week of hard work in dry heat and windy conditions. We slept in old military barracks, and although the work was rewarding, by the time we got back to Georgia, I was exhausted. I began having difficulty breathing and suspected pneumonia again. My doctors in Marietta found fluid on my lungs and first thought it was cancer and not pneumonia. We prayed they were wrong.

Frieda & Charles, Rev. Kimmel – June 8, 1996

CHAPTER 58

You're Having Twins

The doctors at the Emory Transplant Clinic correctly diagnosed the cause of the lung fluid as another case of ascites caused by my deteriorating liver. I was put on powerful diuretics and set up for a new battery of tests to determine my remaining liver function. When the transplant team told me I was finally at the point of needing a liver transplant, it was like a punch in the gut. I had survived an eighteen-year battle with liver disease and now was facing the potential of losing my life if the transplant didn't go well. On the other hand, if all went well, my life could be extended for eighteen or more years into the future. During the medical workup for my transplant, the gastroenterologist made an amazing discovery.

"Congratulations, Mrs. Dixon," he said with a smile on his face. "You are having twins."

"What!" I blurted, as Charles' face turned red.

"You now have two spleens. During your Splenectomy, a piece must have been left behind, and it has regenerated, creating two baby spleens. Your spleen is important in fighting infection, so this is a good thing." I thanked God for his continued goodness to me.

When I asked the doctors at Emory to explain the timing for receiving a transplant, they told me, "You have to be falling off the cliff, and we try to catch you before you land." Not exactly a cheerful thing to consider. What would be my chances of surviving such a risky surgery if I were already critically ill? Their point was that livers were only given to the sickest people as a last resort. Once your old liver is removed, you will live only if the transplanted organ works. We prayed for God's will to be done and for Him to show the doctors how to "catch me before I hit the ground." Signing all the papers allowing the transplant process to go forward was a sobering experience. Once my name was listed on the National Organ Sharing Network, there would be no turning back.

Not only does the patient bear a heavy burden, so do the caregivers. Charles and I, as well as Stuart and Michael, were required to attend psychological counseling. The expectation was that I be totally compliant and committed to taking all the immune suppressing drugs and follow all doctors' orders after my release from the hospital. Charles' commitment involved driving me on the long trek back and forth to Emory several times a week for several months so that my medication levels could be monitored. Our vows to love one another for "better or worse, in sickness and in health" were being put to the test.

CHAPTER 59

~

Audrey's Battle

My sister, Audrey and I shared much over the years. Her encouragement and counseling helped me get through some tough situations. Even though I knew she had many of my symptoms, it still came as a shock to discover that she and I shared not only the DNA that bound us together as biological sisters, but we had each received the aberrant gene that would blossom into full blown liver disease. Little did we know growing up in Burke and Webster that one day we would fight the same battle for survival. She was also diagnosed with PBC but wasn't ready to talk about a transplant for herself. I prayed that she would have many years before she would need one. She felt that since she was eight years older than I was, she might not qualify when the time came.

I was informed in December 1997 that sometime after the first of the year, my name would be placed on the national transplant waiting list, but since I was not yet critical, it probably would take months to find a suitable donor organ. Since that was the case, I urged my doctors at Emory to fix my female issues. A gynecologist at Emory was willing to perform the needed operation after explaining all the difficulties of the elective surgery. I scheduled the surgery for late January 1998— two weeks after my daughter-in-law, Ruth, was due to deliver my second granddaughter.

My best laid plans were turned upside down the first week in January. It was a week I never want to repeat. Earlier than expected, on January 7, I was listed on the National Organ Sharing Network. That same day my daughter-in-law Ruth went into early labor. The delivery of my second granddaughter, Rose, was long, complicated, and dangerous because of Ruth's blood pressure. No sooner did I get that news, than I received word that Audrey had been admitted to the ER with an esophageal bleed or hemorrhage—a very dangerous complication of liver disease. Her life was in jeopardy as the doctors worked to control the bleeding. She lapsed into a coma and was in critical condition for weeks. I decided to postpone my female surgery until Audrey's life was no longer in danger. I had to be available if anything happened to her. Many prayers were said, and God graciously intervened. Ruth delivered a healthy baby girl, and Audrey's life was spared.

My female surgery was rescheduled for mid-February. It involved a lot of abdominal cutting and internal repair. The pain was excruciating for weeks since I was limited in the amount of pain medication I could have due to declining liver function. Three months later, when I was finally on the road to recovery, the call came.

CHAPTER 60

~

Falling Off the Cliff

Tuesday, May 11, 1998, was bright and beautiful. The temperature was in the seventies and I was finally starting to feel like myself again. The long painful recovery from the female surgery was behind me, and I was feeling pretty good. The doctors had removed a lot of tangled scar tissue from my abdomen and agreed that it would make a transplant a lot easier procedure when the time came. Charles had patiently taught me how to use Microsoft Word on the computer, and I was practicing my new skills. The pager that I had been assigned when I was listed for transplant was on my waist. I wore it everywhere I went but didn't expect it to go off anytime soon.

I was expecting a call back from a nurse at Emory about a refill for a medication. When the phone rang, I was surprised to hear the voice of my assigned transplant coordinator instead. I was shocked when she told me a donor liver was available, and I needed to get to Emory Hospital as soon as possible to be prepped for transplant. She said my criteria and that of a donor liver seemed to be a perfect match.

I struggled to believe it was my time to get a new liver and not just a false alarm. I'd heard too many stories about people who were called in for transplant and at the last minute, the surgery was cancelled. If problems with cross matching the blood types or with the health or size of the donated liver were discovered, the potential recipient was sent home to wait for another time.

My hurried trip to the hospital seemed surreal. *Was this really happening?* For eighteen years I had lived with PBC—much longer than anyone expected. *Was the long, arduous battle about to come to an end?* Once I got to the hospital and we approached the time for the surgery with no red flags or stop signs, it appeared that I was indeed about to "fall off the cliff." Now it was up to the transplant surgical team to catch me on the way down.

The science fiction movie, *Deep Impact*, was raking in big bucks at theaters around the country when I was wheeled into the operating room for my transplant. In the movie, a seven-mile-wide comet was expected to impact the earth and cause a mass extinction unless it was destroyed in a race against time. While heaven and earth were about to collide on the silver screen, my life hung between heaven and earth in the surgical suite at Emory Hospital. Only the grace of God and the wonders of modern medicine would determine my fate.

While my second chance at life was in the capable hands of the surgical team, I was oblivious to the events surrounding my transplant. But for my family and friends, it was a different story. After a very poor night of sleep, Charles, Stuart, and Michael faced a long uncertain day. The surgical waiting room at Emory University Hospital was known for its serviceability and not its ambiance. Uncomfortable chairs, worn magazines, and vending machines filled with sweet drinks and salty snacks made up the décor. Throughout the day, family members of other patients were visited by doctors who relayed reports of successful surgeries. Relieved at the news, loved ones gathered their books and crossword puzzles, anxious to leave the colorless waiting room.

For my family, the vigil was just beginning and would last for ten long hours. There was little for them to do but doze, wait, and eat. Charles, Stuart, and Michael took turns going to the cafeteria so someone was available at all times in case a call came from the operating room. My pastor visited sometime during the day, and one or two friends braved the trek across Atlanta through interstate traffic to spend some time with Charles.

During the ten-hour surgery, my husband remained optimistic about the outcome. He was my cheerleader in the months leading up to the transplant. His belief that my body would accept a new liver never wavered. My sons had watched me suffer from liver disease and survive numerous near-death experiences much longer than Charles had. They, too, were ready for me to have a better future. Around four o'clock, my surgeon, Dr. Thomas Heffron, called them to the family waiting room to tell them the surgery was over, and I was headed to recovery.

CHAPTER 61

Plastic Man

With my dry mouth and heavy tongue, I tried to tell Charles, "I am strangling." I helplessly looked into his eyes for some assurance that he understood me. Finally, he held a pad of paper in front of my face and gave me a pen. My foggy brain and shaking hand tried to form the letters of the word "strangling," but as I drifted back to sleep the crooked letters slid down the page.

When I was listed for transplant, I had taken a tour of the intensive care unit at Emory University Hospital. The medical team wanted their patients to know what to expect when they awoke from surgery. Nothing prepared me for the suffocating feeling of claustrophobia I experienced. The whoosh and beeping of machines surrounded me. Numerous bags of fluid were attached to my body with yards of plastic tubing which allowed vital fluids and medicine to drip into my body. My hands were tied to the bed so I couldn't yank out the respirator that was in my throat. A blood pressure cuff on my arm was constantly inflating and deflating as it registered my vital signs. Leg compression cuffs squeezed my legs like a python so clots wouldn't form in my legs. My abdomen was bound in bandages that covered the seventy-five staples that held my incision together.

"You sure are looking good," Charles lied as he gently held my hand. "The doctor says you did real well. Your face is pink." My face color for some time had been gray with a tint of yellow or green, but definitely not pink. With the respirator in my throat, I was unable to speak. Stuart, Michael, and our pastor quietly entered my room to see for themselves that I had survived the ordeal. We worked out a communication code—one blink meant "yes," and two blinks meant "no."

I was warned by the transplant team of the effects of the medication that would surge through my veins. Massive doses of steroids and immune-suppressing drugs were vital so that my body would accept the foreign organ. The possible side effects of those medications were paranoia and psychosis, among other things. By the second night in ICU, my dreams had turned vivid and scary. "Plastic Man" was spinning long plastic tubes out of his fingers, wrapping me up like a bug in a spider's web, and coming to eat me for lunch. I woke up in a drenching sweat.

By the third day, my respirator was removed, and I could drink water and other liquids. But that also meant I had to swallow a vile tasting medicine concoction that I promptly threw up. That immune-suppressant drug had to be retained before I could get out of ICU. Once I could eat solid food, it became easier to get it down. Then I was expected to swallow the drug in five horse-sized capsules that smelled as bad as the liquid had tasted. All the nurses assured me I would get used to taking them. As soon as I left ICU and arrived in a private room, I was required to learn the schedule for taking all my drugs. I was responsible for swallowing around 30 pills each day, and they all had to be on a certain schedule—some before food, some with food, and others in between. It was mind boggling, but I was determined to master my meds and do four laps around the nurses' station so I could go home.

My recuperation from the extensive surgery was uneventful and right on schedule. All the medical personnel agreed that I was very fortunate to not have any rejection or infection issues during the first few days post-op. I had a vivid dream during my last night in the hospital.

Several of my deceased loved ones, including Talmadge and my parents, were all leaning over a low wall in heaven looking down on me in my hospital bed. They all wore big smiles and were showing "thumbs up" and saying, "Good job, Fifi Minnow. We knew you could do it."

As I left the hospital eleven days after surgery, I thought about the journey I had taken and the people who had walked with me every step of the way. Many family members and friends had stood by me and helped me get through my eighteen-year ordeal. I was humbled by God's overwhelming grace that had allowed me to still occupy space on His earth. I felt so undeserving and yet so grateful for all my blessings. It was a joy to go back home to Kennesaw and sit on the back porch swing, listen to the wind rustle the leaves of the trees, and watch the birds fight for space on the bird feeder.

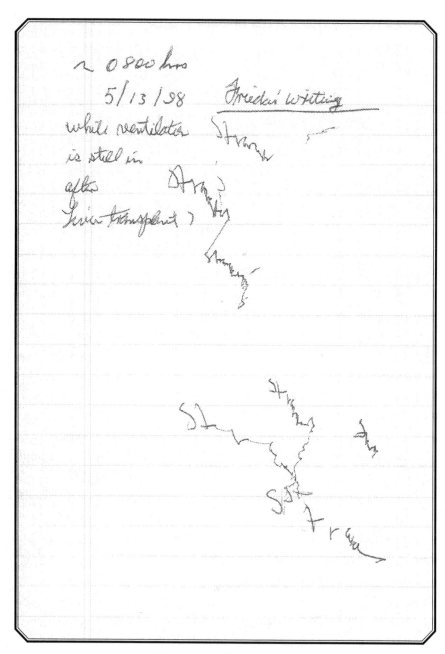

Post-transplant Scribble

CHAPTER 62

Dear Donor Family

Constant itching was the most miserable symptom I had experienced during the years I had lived with liver disease. After my transplant, I no longer itched day and night. That relief should have helped my sleep, but sleep was very elusive. The large doses of steroids coursing through my veins made me a nervous wreck and kept me from falling and staying asleep. Most nights I stared at the ceiling while my husband was sound asleep next to me. I felt like I was still attached to an IV with hi-test caffeine dripping into my veins. The steroids increased my appetite, and I couldn't get enough to eat. My thin, frail body responded well to the requirement that I eat a lot of nourishing food.

Charles was the best nurse anyone could have, but he was still trying to work on his Lockheed contract and couldn't be at home all the time. Friends and church members took turns bringing in food and taking shifts staying with me until I was three weeks post-transplant. I was amazed by everyone's generosity, love, and prayers.

Rejection and infection are the two enemies of a transplanted liver. Powerful drugs to prevent rejection have to be delicately balanced so the body does not become vulnerable to fungal and bacterial infections. I had to be very careful around people who might be carrying flu or cold viruses, especially my grandchildren. Changing diapers and digging in the dirt were two major restrictions for all transplant patients.

While my body was fighting to accept and not reject the foreign liver that was now nestled under my right rib cage, a family was dealing with their own personal grief. My family was buoyed by hope for a better future while my donor family was making funeral arrangements. My donor's life had been cut short, but my life had been extended. Since only healthy organs are transplanted, my donor most likely had been in the prime of life.

As soon as I was able to collect my thoughts, I wrote an anonymous letter to the family of my donor. The National Organ Sharing Network (NOSN) requires that donors and recipients not reveal their identities, much like adoptions. But we could send a letter to the network, and they would send the letter to the donor family. Six weeks after receiving my gift of life, I penned the following letter:

June 22, 1998
Dear Donor Family,

Six weeks ago I received a second chance at life. The generosity of your family at the time of the loss of your loved one restored my life. You are really to be admired for making such an important decision at such a difficult time.

Every day I thank God for my new liver, and I pray for your family and grieve with you in the death of your loved one. Even though our paths may never cross, we will always share a common bond that links us together.

For 18 years, I lived with liver disease and it greatly affected my ability to live a full life. This past year, in particular, was very hard since I stayed exhausted and was getting sicker all the time. All that changed on May 11 when the call came for my transplant. I have done very well since the transplant and now have hope for a long, bright future. I have a husband, two married sons, and two beautiful granddaughters, with a grandson on the way. Now I will have a chance to be "Grammy" for years to come.

I know every day is filled with the memories of the one you lost. I pray that God will make those only the most beautiful memories and that He will ease the pain you experience.

Thank you again for myself, my family, and friends who have walked through this experience with me and who share your loss as well.

Sincerely,
A grateful liver recipient

CHAPTER 63

The Gift of Life

I felt very fortunate to receive the following response from my donor family, who wrote to me in the midst of their grief and loss. Her sister wrote on behalf of the family and introduced me to the girl whose death gave me a second chance at life. Some information has been deleted to protect the privacy of my donor family.

August 13, 1998

Dear Liver Recipient:

We are so glad that our dearly departed daughter/sister could help you live your life a little stronger and healthier. *** our daughter/sister, was a caring person. She had an outgoing personality and enjoyed family and friends. We didn't know how many friends she had until she passed away. They kept coming. That was nice to see. I'm telling you this hoping that you will keep your family and friends close as you never know when your time is up.

A little about ***. She was very petite, 100 pounds average. She was the third child of four. Both her parents and her three siblings are still living. She also has two nephews and two nieces. She was not married (divorced) and had no children. She died from complications stemming from a one-car accident. No one knows what happened, whether an animal ran out in front of her and she tried to avoid it, or she fell asleep (it was around 11:00 p.m.), or something else, we don't know.

*** loved playing softball. She was right-handed, but batted left handed. She was fast. She usually led off the batting and could do a good "softball" bunt! She also like to fish. The day of her accident, she and Daddy went fishing. He will forever treasure that time they spent together. She was taking some of those fish to her aunt (after she picked up a friend to go with her), but never made it to the friend's house.*** lived in ***. Both parents and two sisters do also. Her accident was about 30 miles from home.

We have all struggled with this tragedy in our family. All our family deaths have been from old age. We do feel a small sigh of relief that *** death wasn't a complete loss. Knowing you are doing better, even though we don't know you, is comforting. *** never had an opportunity to really help someone, but in death, she did. I am *** sister (I'm the youngest) and I am writing on behalf of *** whole family.

We would like to correspond with you to keep up with your progress and meet you when you feel comfortable with that. We will keep you and your family in our prayers, and we hope you will do the same for us.

Sincerely,
***

I tried to arrange a meeting through the National Organ Sharing Network between me and my donor family. The NOSN discouraged that initiative, believing that anonymity was best for all concerned.

I learned on one of my follow-up visits to Emory that someone else was supposed to have received my donor's liver, but that person had become too critically ill to qualify. Even though I was not in the hospital and waiting, the decision had been made not to waste the organ. The transplant surgeon later told me that the donor liver had been a perfect match for my body. He grinned as he said, "Your initials were written on that liver." It was very sobering to realize that two people had died before I had been given a second chance at life.

I often prayed for my donor family and wondered why my life had been spared and hers had been lost. I thought about my many years of liver disease and why the best years of my life had been given over to physical suffering. Those were the same types of issues people had been grappling with for hundreds of years. I surely didn't have all the answers, but I chose to place my unanswered questions into the safekeeping of an all-wise and loving God.

CHAPTER 64

A New Millennium

During 1998 a huge burden had been lifted from my life. For the first time in years, I felt hope for a normal life and many years to enjoy it. Even though I still had days when I didn't feel well, my health was no longer declining. It was on an upward trajectory.

Audrey's condition, however, remained a dark cloud on my otherwise sunny horizon. After surviving a second esophageal hemorrhage, she was placed on the transplant waiting list and remained hospitalized until a suitable liver could be found. Charles drove me to Gainesville, Florida to visit her in the hospital. I was shocked to see her in such a weakened state. She finally received her transplant on November 12, 1998, six months to the day after mine. Her recovery did not go well, and she developed a massive yeast infection that almost took her life. She was left with severe damage to one of her retinas, leaving her legally blind. Gradually, she crawled back to some measure of health, but then she found out that the PBC had returned in her new liver.

At the end of 1999 everyone was anticipating the close of the twentieth century and the beginning of the twenty-first. As the century and the millennium wound down, it was a time of great anticipation as well as fear. Roughly six billion people were alive on December 31, 1999 when fireworks exploded around the world to welcome in the new millennium.

Many had been fearful of what was called Y2K, the nickname given to the anticipated massive computer meltdowns. It was thought by many that computer-dependent technologies would crash as the calendar turned from one century to the next, and that the world would be plunged into darkness. People stockpiled food, water, batteries, and built Y2K shelters to protect themselves from the inevitable looting. Charles and I decided it was overblown hype, so we planned a Y2K party to welcome in the millennium. As we said goodbye to the twentieth century, I said goodbye to a very eventful and challenging fifty-five years of life. American author and columnist Bill Vaughn once said, "An optimist stays up until midnight to see the New Year in. A pessimist stays up to make sure the old year leaves." With God's help, I was ready to face the future with optimism and hope.

~

Afterword

As I reflect on the years of my life, I am amazed and thankful that with God's help I survived and overcame many obstacles. I am also amazed that God gave me so many second chances that I did not deserve. Left to my own strength and resources, I would have failed miserably to live my life in a meaningful way. All that changed when I became a believer in Jesus Christ at age twenty-one. That decision ushered in a new era for me. Jesus became my Savior, companion, and friend. He walked with me, and at times carried me, through the turmoil of my young and middle adulthood. A second chance at marriage wasn't even on my radar screen, yet I was provided with a loving partner in Charles. As if that weren't enough, I received a third chance at life itself and the opportunity to reclaim the years I had lost to death and disease. I was truly *Born Three Times*.

The years since the turn of the millennium have been good and mostly healthy ones. I did experience one episode of organ rejection in 2000, but that was quickly reversed by a change in medication. My doctors are pleased that I have done so well since then and often tell me, "Now you get to have the aches and pains of old age just like the rest of us." My sister, Jan, died of heart failure in 2000. I still miss her outspoken personality. Audrey's quality of life post-transplant has greatly improved. We took a trip to the mountains to celebrate our mutual ten-year transplant anniversary in 2008.

Charles and I have worked diligently to build up our aerospace company, Consulting Aviation Services. Full retirement is still elusive because of the demands of our business. We have welcomed more grandchildren and great-grandchildren into our family. I have discovered a great desire to write and have had some success in getting stories published and winning recognition in writing contests. We continue to serve as God leads through our church and in our community.

My cranberry glass collection is still proudly displayed in my curio cabinet. The shimmering gold I see in each piece is a reminder of God's past, present, and future work in my life. When Jesus delivered his prophecy to the apostle John, as found written in the book of Revelation, He admonished him, "I counsel you to buy from me gold refined in the fire, so that you can become rich…" (Revelation 3:18). These words have new meaning to me as I remember my many years in the "refiner's fire" and how God worked in my life to bring me through. He has indeed made me rich.

"But he knows the way that I take; and when he has tested me,
I will come forth as gold" (Job 23:10).

—Frieda Dixon